What Are You Waiting For?

BOOKS IN THE PROTESTANT PULPIT EXCHANGE

What Are You Waiting For?

Sermons on the
Parables of Jesus

Mark Trotter

Abingdon Press
Nashville

WHAT ARE YOU WAITING FOR? SERMONS ON THE PARABLES OF JESUS

This book is printed on recycled, acid-free paper.

Trotter, Mark.
    What are you waiting for? : sermons on the parables of Jesus /
Mark Trotter.
        p.   cm. — (Protestant pulpit exhange)
    ISBN 0-687-44604-X (pbk. : alk. paper)
    1. Jesus Christ—Parables—Sermons.   2. Methodist Church—Sermons.
3. Sermons, American.   I. Title.   II. Series.
BT375.2.T76   1992
252'.076—dc20   92-20954
                                                                    CIP

Scripture quotations, unless otherwise indicated, are from the New
Revised Standard Version Bible, copyright © 1989, by the Division of
Christian Education of the National Council of the Churches of Christ in
the United States of America.

"Long Live the Weeds," copyright 1936 by Theodore Roethke. From THE
COLLECTED POEMS OF THEODORE ROETHKE by Theodore
Roethke. Used by permission of Doubleday, a division of Bantam Double-
day Dell Publishing Group, Inc.

"Finding Is the First Act," by Emily Dickerson, is from The Complete Poems of
Emily Dickinson, Thomas H. Johnson, editor, Little Brown & Co, 1960.
Used by permission.

MANUFACTURED IN THE UNITED STATES OF AMERICA

For
Jean

Contents

Introduction

*I*n seminary in the late fifties I had the impression that all the serious work in biblical studies had been done. The Germans, and a few Britishers, had wrapped it up, and nothing more need be said.

I also concluded that biblical scholarship wouldn't be much help to me as a preacher. I found Form Criticism, the reigning school at the time, interesting and useful in teaching, but unconcerned with the meaning of a text. It seemed preoccupied with the classification of literary forms. In addition there was an implied value judgment on the historical validity of various forms which left the preacher with the impression that there was precious little left to preach.

Though I was still determined to be what was called in those days a "biblical" preacher, I turned out to be just another "topical" preacher, using the biblical text for illustrations, not for interpretation.

Then came the revolution called "the new literary criticism" and I found myself having to relearn everything I had been taught in seminary. I had been taught to approach biblical literature as historical documents. We attempted to get at what really happened, so that those documents closest to the event were the most reliable (e.g., Mark), those coming later less reliable (e.g., John). The new literary criticism approached the Gospels as literature and therefore to be understood not only by historical context, but by employing the rules of literary analysis. The text was no longer seen as an historical artifact, the value of which was determined by its date in the past. It was now seen as literature, placed in the canon because of its value in interpreting the present. No longer did one Gospel have priority over another, but all were equally "gospel," or different testimonies to the same event.

Since that "awakening" I have tried to read as much literary criticism as I can. Some of it reads like esoterica, but some is like finding the map to a treasure. As a result my preaching has changed, and continues to evolve, and I expect now that it always will because of the multivalency of texts made possible by the new criticism.

My first exposure to the new criticism came through the writings of the American parable scholars, most of whom are students of, or indebted to, Amos Wilder. From them we have learned what a parable does as literature. It is not a homey illustration of a familiar truth but a "metaphor," opening new ways of seeing the world and thereby upsetting conventional wisdom and piety.

This book is heavily in debt to a study of the parables by Bernard Brandon Scott entitled *Hear Then the Parable* (1989), especially his thesis that Jesus' parables contain *mythemes*, or traditional cultural values preserved in story form used by Jesus as the raw material for his stories. As a result Jesus' parables begin like conventional rabbinic stories, and sound like them, but at some point turn 180 degrees and end up as something quite different.

Not all parables follow that formula. Other scholars caution us that some of Jesus' stories, particularly those that warn, are straightforward. Still, preachers should look first for the mytheme, the conventional pattern, and expect a reversal.

I am also indebted to the redaction critics who emphasized that the Gospel writers were not mere anthologists of anecdotal material, or historians working in a pre-scientific age, but gifted writers with a point of view and a message to get across. The pericopes have an intentional order and have been edited with a theological intention. Therefore, the Gospels are stories to be read as a whole, each passage interpreted as part of the whole. The most persistent reminder of the importance of this order for preaching comes from Fred Craddock, most helpfully in his book, *The Gospels*.

This journey through the last twenty or so years of biblical studies has left me with the following assumptions:

1) The Church is the audience for the Gospels, especially when the disciples are addressed in the text: "Then Jesus called his disciples to him and said . . ."

2) The "crowd" is different than the "disciples." Jesus ministered to the crowd, fed them, healed them, performed miracles for them. The disciples (Church) were not so much ministered to as called to minister.

3) The Gospels are interpretation. Matthew is interpreting for his generation the tradition handed to him. Our task is not to repeat Matthew's interpretation but find the tradition in Matthew's text and interpret it anew for our time.

4) Parables are metaphors. Although scholars argue over this, they agree that Jesus generally emphasized a metaphorical use as a means to see something we do not now have the eyes to see. This is the single most important assumption for contemporary preaching. Parables ought to do for us what they did for those who first heard them.

5. In Matthew's situation, the proclamation of grace was being misused, which resulted in a lessening of moral standards. Perhaps this problem is analogous to the situation in Paul's churches where spiritual gifts were being used to justify immoral and un-Christian behavior. So Matthew stresses Christianity's relationship to Judaism, especially its moral heritage. Matthew uses typology liberally to help the reader know that the New Covenant is to be understood in terms of the Old Covenant. Jesus climbs a mountain recapitulating Moses'

ascent of Sinai to receive the Law. That critical passage (chapters 5-7) along with typologies of the Exodus, are there to emphasize that the heart of Judaism, its covenant rooted in righteousness, holds for the Christian. We see this use of the Old Covenant especially in the parables of judgment.

These chapters were originally delivered as sermons to the people of the First United Methodist Church of San Diego. I am most grateful to them. There is no finer congregation of hearers. They come to worship expecting something to happen, something surprising, a palpable readiness felt by the preacher immediately upon entering the pulpit.

My special thanks to Shirley McKim, who labored through several drafts to complete a readable manuscript, and who at critical points offered valuable suggestions.

CHAPTER ONE

> Listen! A sower went out to sow. And as he sowed, some seeds fell on
> the path, and the birds came and ate them up. Other seeds fell on
> rocky ground, where they did not have much soil, and they sprang up
> quickly, since they had no depth of soil. But when the sun rose, they
> were scorched; and since they had no root, they withered away. Other
> seeds fell among thorns, and the thorns grew up and choked them.
> Other seeds fell on good soil and brought forth grain, some a hundred-
> fold, some sixty, some thirty. Let anyone with
> ears listen! Matthew 13:1-9, 18-23

The Sower

I try to live my life efficiently. I order it rationally, put
everything in its proper place, schedule my activities systematically. My goal is to "plan my work and work my
plan." I find that it is easier to do that while pulling
weeds than when running a church. I start at one end of the
garden and systematically work my way down to the other
end, eliminating every weed in sight. When I finish I stand
up, look back, and proudly say, "Well done, good and faithful
servant." It's hard work, but when I'm finished I have
brought some order into an otherwise disorderly world.

There are other areas of life where efficiency pays off.
Henry Ford discovered the profitability of efficiency and
transformed American industry with the assembly line. The
assembly line was simply the application of rationality to the
process of production. The process was divided into units,
each unit given a task, and the work force divided corre-
spondingly. The final product was an automobile produced
with the maximum speed at the minimum cost.

Efficiency probably reached its zenith with the McDonald's hamburger. The same method was applied. The process of making a hamburger was analyzed rationally, the elements isolated, down to the actual arm movements, the number of steps, required to assemble a hamburger for a customer. A few seconds were saved here, and a few there. The result was a low cost meal served in the minimum amount of time. McDonald's is an amazing success story, and it can be told as the story of efficiency.

Efficiency in America has become so important that there arises a social class called "managers" who can go into any organization and run it efficiently. They assume that the rules of efficiency are universal. It doesn't matter what the organization is, what its purpose is, or what it produces—the principles are similar and universal.

Almost. There are some limits to rational management. H. L. Mencken said, "There is an easy solution to every human problem—neat, plausible and wrong." Which fact I discovered when I became the father of a family of four small children. It was then I came to see that the rational model of the world may have some limitations. Robert Capon describes children as gifts to us to remind us that beneath the rational orderliness that we impose on the world, there lies a primordial chaos. "Whatever order I was able to bring into my house was like a ripple on the surface of a vast ocean, and beneath it, in the depth, remained an unfathomable mystery."

Robert Capon, himself the father of six children, described what happened in his household at mealtime. After the grace, the table became chaos, a frenzy of noise and movement. He finally shouted, "Quiet!"

Its's a pretty negative approach, but it works. In the shuffling stillness, the hint of order comes again. I quote them St. Paul on the subject of pots talking back to the potter. (I remind them that they are civilized. They are not a mob, and therefore, manners are expected.) The older ones agree. I am encouraged. Then the youngest knocks over a glass of milk. Down toward me it races, like a flood across the land. I jump up and back, but over the edge it pours. And I am hit, right trouser leg below the knee. It's the third time this meal. My largesse is nothing next to the cataract of milk she has produced in three short years. And my inventiveness is small. She has spilled it backhand, forehand, sidearm, elbow first. She has upset glasses with her head, her feet, her shoulders, her knees, her rump, her belly, the middle of her back. And with an endless variety of time and circumstance. Upon thick tablecloths yielding a white swamp which spreads ominously toward us all. Upon plastic tablecloths for a high velocity attack. I can remember only one successful escape from milk on plastic. I nearly broke the chair to do it. She has spilled it before, during, after meals by commission and by omission and with enough broken glass to rival the divine scattering of the hoarfrost.[2]

During those years of early parenthood, I would return to that passage in Capon's book for perspective. It reminded me that efficiency is an arbitrary structure that we impose upon the surface of existence. In fact, it can be done only by circumscribing some fragment of experience, such as assembling automobiles or making hamburgers, and imposing it there. But other areas of life will always defy rational analysis and organization. The more human beings are involved, the less it works. The more you try to make human beings conform to some rational model, the more damage you do.

> "*Efficiency is an arbitrary structure that we impose upon the surface of existence.*"

Sometimes in counseling he will say, "She doesn't understand reason." Or she will say, "He thinks he is so rational, why does he do such dumb things?" I tell them, "The first thing you have to realize is that you are not married to a rational being. You are married to a human being, who has rational capacities to a lesser and greater degree, but who, beneath the surface, is emotional, irrational, sometimes crazy, and always a mystery. You are living with a human being, and treating her as if she were a hamburger just isn't going to work."

I would say that where things really matter, such as in human relationships, it doesn't work at all. Love works there. Nor in overcoming adversity. Hope works better there. Nor in understanding the hard questions of life. Faith is what will work there. If you try to impose a rational model on those areas of existence, you will end up frustrated and probably angry.

In Judith Guest's novel, *Ordinary People,* there is a marvelous description of the father of a family. His two sons are involved in a boating accident in which one son drowns. The incident devastates the family. The surviving son lives the rest of his life with guilt. The mother covers her grief with busyness. The father sinks into despair. He is described in these words:

> He had left off being a perfectionist then when he discovered that no promptly kept appointments, not a house circumspectly clean, not membership in Onwentsia, or the Lake Forest Golf and Country Club, or the Lawyers' Club. Not power, not knowledge, not goodness, not anything, cleared you through the terrifying office of chance. And that it is chance, and not perfection, that rules the world.[3]

Those who believe they are rational beings can organize their lives efficiently in some areas of their life, sometimes with spectacular results. When all experience does not respond to rational ordering and understanding, they resent it, and end up in bitterness, guilt, or despair.

We can order existence rationally to a degree, the way we can push back the sea a little with a dike, or stop a river for a while with a dam. But beyond the boundaries reason constructs there is disorder, mystery, and even chaos. And sometimes that other world seeps from under the dike, or during a storm overflows the dam, to flood our lives with absurdity. When that happens there is nothing we can do except let it recede. Our technology can't control it. Our reason can't explain it. Our efficiency can't contain it.

The Parable of the Sower addresses this dilemma. Matthew has interpreted the parable to answer questions raised by the early Church. Namely, if Jesus is the Messiah, then why isn't everybody converted? If the Kingdom of God is here, why doesn't the world look like it? Why hasn't the Church been more successful in its mission?

Those hard questions were demanding an answer, and Matthew used The Parable of the Sower as an answer. He recorded the parable as Jesus told it (Matthew 13:3-9), then interpreted it for his situation (Matthew 13:18-23). That's why there are two versions of The Parable of the Sower in the thirteenth chapter.

Actually, Matthew's interpretation (13:18-23) turns the parable into an allegory where each type of soil represents a certain type of person. It was an appropriate application for the parable to the first-century Church, making sense of their situation, and giving the Church hope. It is not as helpful for us. So we will follow Matthew's example and interpret the original parable (13:3-9) for our time.

One meaning of the parable is found by seeing yourself as the sower. Let the seed that is broadcast widely represent your effort to live a meaningful life in this world, the things that you have tried to do, our labor at making a living, or raising a family, your investment in doing something worthwhile with your life. Those deeds are like seed that you have sown, some of which succeed and some of which don't. Sometimes the seed falls on good ground. Sometimes it falls amidst the rocks and the thorns.

The parable calls you to be realistic. You win some and you lose some. You experience victory and you know defeat. You have good days and you have bad days. One day life gives, the next it takes away. In other words, you can control what you do but you can't always control the results of what you do. Sometimes, no matter how hard you work, no matter how sincere you are, no matter how efficient you are, you are not going to succeed. So do your best. Sow the seed and leave the rest to God.

That's one simple message of the parable. But implied in the parable is this question: If life is that way, why do you persist in expecting success from all of your efforts? There is nothing in your "contract" that guarantees you success. In fact, there is no contract at all. Porky, in the "Pogo" comic strip, put it perfectly to Churchy La Femme after listening to him for four frames complain about the condition of the world: "Shut up. You are lucky to be here in the first place." When you begin with the assumption that life offers no guarantee of success, then maybe you can see that what you have is not necessarily the results of your efforts.

The parable is trying to get you to see your life in a new way. It does not explain why things go wrong, why there are infertile, unproductive soils. In the Bible, evil isn't explained; it remains a mystery. The parable assumes that some things will go wrong. Not all the seeds will take root. That's the way life is.

> "The parable assumes that some things will go wrong. Not all the seeds will take root. That's the way life is."

Therefore the question could just as well be, Why do things go right? Don't ask, Why is there evil in the world? Or why is there so much injustice in human events? Ask, Why do some things succeed? Where do good things come from? Not from our ability to guarantee success. Not from our efforts at efficiency. Our efforts are like sowing seed, inefficient. Some fall on good soil, some on bad. Some things in your control will fail, other things will succeed. And sometimes, beyond our imagining, and always beyond our deserving, some seed will take root and grow. That's the point: You are the sower, that's all. You can do only so much, and you will succeed only so often. God is in charge of the rest.

Henri Nouwen, a Dutch priest and theologian, spent a year in Bolivia and Peru. In an interview he talked about what he learned about himself.

I came to realize there that being a Western, Northern person, you always want to do something, you always want to have a plan. You see problems and you want to change something. We have a very structured kind of thinking. Well, when I got there I soon realized if I wanted to approach reality that way I might as well give up. When I walked from the church to home, which was twenty minutes up the hill over a sandy, dusty road, the little children would come up to me and take me by the fingers, literally, so that I didn't have any free fingers left. They climbed all over my body and they were always around me, looking at me, playing with me, playing ball around me. They were telling me something: they were giving me a sense of "This is the day the Lord has made; let us celebrate; let us be glad; let's just be aware of each other." They were indirectly unmasking my illusion of wanting to do something big; they kept laughing and playing and telling me something about life that I didn't know. In the midst of all the misery and hunger and difficulty there was a life-giving reality.[4]

The Parable of the Sower indicates that there is a life-giving power beyond your power. To be a Christian, to be a person of faith, is to trust that though you aren't in complete control, there is a power in this world that is. No matter how hard you try, you are not going to be able to bring order into mystery. You are not going to get rid of chaos. You are not creator. You are a sower of seed, that's all. Some will fall on good soil, and some will fall among the thorns and the rocks. So do your best, and trust the rest to God.

CHAPTER TWO

> *The kingdom of heaven may be compared to someone who sowed good seed in his field; but while everybody was asleep, an enemy came and sowed weeds among the wheat, and then went away. So when the plants came up and bore grain, then the weeds appeared as well. And the slaves of the householder came and said to him, "Master, did you not sow good seed in your field? Where, then, did these weeds come from?" He answered, "An enemy has done this." The slaves said to him, "Then do you want us to go and gather them?" But he replied, "No; for in gathering the weeds you would uproot the wheat along with them. Let both of them grow together until the harvest; and at harvest time I will tell the reapers, 'Collect the weeds first and bind them in bundles to be burned, but gather the wheat into my barn.'"*
> *Matthew 13:24-30*

The Wheat and Tares

A farmer who discovered weeds among the wheat in his field said, "An enemy has done this." I wonder what that means? I am not aware of having any enemies myself. An enemy has done this? Is that a clue to this parable?

As was the case with The Parable of the Sower, The Parable of the Wheat and Tares appears in two versions. First Matthew records Jesus' original parable (Matthew 13:24-30), then converts it to an allegory to interpret it for that church's situation (Matthew 13:36-43). As an allegory, the good seed refers to the sons of the kingdom; the bad seed equals the sons of the

20

evil one. The sower is the Son of man; the enemy is the devil. The harvest is the close of the age; the reapers are the angels. The allegorical interpretation spoke to Matthew's congregation, and it could make sense for your situation, but we will go back to the original parable (13:24-30) to find a message for our time.

A farmer is meticulous about his farming. He tries to be the very best farmer that he can. He has a good field in which to work. He sows the highest quality seed, rents the finest equipment, and works hard. In other words, he does everything right. He lives the kind of life that is supposed to produce dramatic results. If the world is fair at all, and if fairness has any meaning at all, then this farmer is exactly the kind who ought to prosper and succeed.

But on the night that he completed the sowing of his high quality seed in this perfectly plowed field, with the contours, geometrically pleasing to the eye, like a Grant Wood painting, while he was sleeping an enemy sowed the seed of a weed in his perfect field. It was done so expertly, so cleverly, that it was not discovered until months later when the workers reported the presence of weeds among the wheat.

A weed in the Middle East, called "darnel," looks just like wheat in the blade. It is indistinguishable as a weed until the ear and the full grain appear. By then it's too late to do anything about it, because the roots of the darnel will have intertwined with the roots of the wheat, so you cannot pull out one without pulling out the other. So when the servant asks, "Do you want us to pull out these weeds?" the master says, "No, let them grow. When the harvest comes both the wheat and the weeds will be cut down and then they will be separated."

The first fascinating insight in this brilliant parable can be gained simply by looking at the context. Matthew 13 is loaded with parables, many of them parables of growth. The Parable of the Sower is placed before this parable; the Parable of the Mustard Seed immediately follows. Both are parables of growth, proclaiming that God is in charge, not us. As any good farmer knows, there's only so much you can do, and you have to leave the rest to God. Sandwiched between the Sower and the Mustard Seed, two parables of growth, is The Parable of the Wheat and Tares, obviously bearing the same message.

> *"As any good farmer knows, there's only so much you can do, and you have to leave the rest to God."*

It's a hard lesson for those of us who, like the farmer in the story, work hard to be successful. To be a success you've got to make sure you have the very best of everything: the best seed, the best equipment, the best land, and you have to work hard. Finally, there must be no margin for error, no room for mistakes, no possibility for things to go awry.

But they do, usually, eventually, almost always. Why do these things happen to me? I did everything right. I went out of my way to make sure that everything was set up just right. It's as if when we are asleep some enemy sows weeds in these beautiful plans of ours, these dreams that we've worked so hard to achieve, this business into which we've invested so much of ourself and money, this family, this relationship, this marriage, this partnership, this friendship. Something happens, and it turns sour, or stale, or flat, or sorrowful. What happened? We've all asked that. What happened?

Sometimes there is an answer, but if so, it is still as if some enemy has done this. Even though we may be able to look into the past and say, "See, here it is, this is the cause," it is still not our doing, not intentionally. We didn't mean it to be like this. We didn't see what was happening until it was too late. We didn't want it to happen. So it's still as if some enemy has done this.

So what can we do? It should be stressed that often you can do something. Churches are in the reclamation business. They help people fix their lives and renew their relationships. The healing professions exist for the same purpose. So it should be said, a lot of these things can be fixed, and you ought to try. But some can't be, and you just have to accept that. When you have done all that you can, that's all you can do, and that's all you are expected to do.

In parables about growth, God is in charge, not you. You can do some things, but you can't do everything, and you can't fix everything. Having done all that you can, can you now trust that in God's time, and in God's providence, this dilemma will work out?

A second insight is similar to the assumption beneath the Parable of the Sower, that this is an imperfect world, and we can't do anything about it. It's a world in which there are weeds, some of them with burrs and stickers, some with toxins and poisons. Weeds are an appropriate symbol of evil in the world. They are persistent, tenacious, and ubiquitous. Weeds are everywhere. There are weeds even in the perfect suburban garden.

Philosophers have tried to explain the presence of evil in the world. You can find their books in the library. There's even a special discipline in theology with its own name that focuses on answers to evil. It's called "Theodicy." Volumes have been written on the question, Why is there evil? In the one place where you would expect to find some answers—the Bible—we uncover virtual silence. According to some scholars, Job is the only biblical book that focuses on the problem of evil, and Job's concludes that human suffering is a mystery.

In the New Testament this parable comes close to a discussion of the question, Why are there weeds in the field? Why is there evil in the world? "An enemy has done this." That's all. Which at least means that God didn't do it. It is not part of the Creation. It's not God's intention that these things should happen. It's God's intention that the field should be perfect. That's all it says—"The owner didn't do this, some enemy is to blame."

For many people that's sufficient, that's enough. To know that God doesn't intend this to happen is sufficient for them to have hope, and courage, and trust that somehow, in God's providence, it will work out.

One purpose of the parable is to give advice on dealing with evil in an imperfect world. Don't be overzealous in eradicating evil, or you will end up doing more harm than good. If you want the evidence, just recall all the crusades in history to wipe out evil, or to get the infidel, or to stamp out the sinner. They all result in the innocent suffering as much as, if not more than anybody else. The roots of the good and the bad are so intertwined that if you try to pull up the one, you are going to pull up the other.

> *"Don't be overzealous in eradicating evil, or you will end up doing more harm than good."*

The so-called Gulf War was designed to eradicate an evil, pull up a noxious weed from Kuwait, eliminate it surgically, as it were, with the miracle of precision armament technology. The mission suceeded in its limited goal, but tens of thousands of people were killed, and thousands more will die and suffer because of it. And the land is devastated. Pulling out weeds may be necessary, but we should weigh the cost to the innocent as well as to the guilty before we do it. In an imperfect world, the innocent are going to suffer as well as the guilty.

No one spoke more eloquently about this than Boris Pasternak, whose novel, *Dr. Zhivago,* is a protest against what he called "fanatical men of action with their one-track minds." The 1927 Bolshevik revolution in Russia was an attempt to pull out the evil of a corrupt monarchy, which it succeeded in doing, but it also issued forth the Soviet Union, a charnel house and a wasteland. The revolution was intended to bring in a new world, but it made the old world worse.

The world is imperfect. We don't know why. We know that our efforts to make it perfect will render it worse. Perhaps that's why Jesus rejected all proposals to make the Kingdom come by force. Violence hurts the innocent as well as the evil. It pulls up the wheat as well as the weeds.

When Derek Bok was President of Harvard University he was asked about his expectations for students who would receive a Harvard education. He said, "Tolerance for ambiguity." That is not a bad summary of the purpose of this parable. Bok went on to explain that in this kind of a world, some problems are so complex that the most you can hope for is different opinions from people of integrity rather than a clear delineation of who is right and who is wrong.

In an imperfect world, certainty is hard to come by, especially certainty about other people. We should let the weeds grow along with the wheat because we do not know enough to judge other people. We don't know what are weeds and what is wheat, not until the harvest. Jesus cautioned us repeatedly, "Judge not that you be not judged." "Take the mote out of your own eye before you take the speck out of somebody else's eye." And to a crowd ready to stone a woman taken in adultery he said, "Let him who is without sin cast the first stone." Because the fact is, none of us know enough to judge another person.

The Indian poet Tagore told of the day his servant arrived at work late. Like so many of his class, Tagore was helpless when it came to menial things, or he made himself helpless because as a member of the upper caste he considered himself to be above these things.

An hour went by and the servant hadn't arrived. Tagore was getting more angry by the minute. He thought of all the punishments he was going to inflict upon his servant when he arrived. Three hours passed. Now he was no longer thinking of punishments, he knew that he would summarily fire him when he finally appeared.

At noon the servant came to work. Without a word, he proceeded to do his chores, picking up his master's clothes, making his meal, and doing other chores around the house. Tagore watched all of this in silent rage. He finally said, "Drop everything and get out of here. You're fired." The man kept working, quietly, diligently. Tagore said, "Get out of here." The man said, "My little girl died this morning."

That story reminds us that we do not know what goes on in other people's lives. We do not know the burdens that other people carry. In America we like to talk about tolerance. We consider it to be part of the spirit of America. The real basis for tolerance is our mutual ignorance. You don't know what problems others live with. You don't know what they have resisted as well as what they have committed. You don't know what is weed and what is wheat until the harvest, and if you happen to be there, you may be surprised.

Here is still another insight. We are to let the weeds and the wheat grow together because God is not finished yet. That's the good news of the parable: God isn't finished yet. Most of us have lived long enough to see good come out of evil: God isn't finished yet. Or we have seen something that we were sure was the worst thing to happen turn out to be the best thing that could happen. Not only that, we have seen what we were sure was evil, even a so-called "evil empire," change overnight and become democracies: God isn't finished yet.

That's the message of this poem by Theodore Roethke.

> Long live the weeds that overwhelm
> My narrow vegetable realm!
> The bitter rock, the barren soil
> That force the son of man to toil;
> All things unholy, marred by curse,
> The ugly of the universe.

The rough, the wicked and the wild
That keeps the spirit undefiled.
With these I match my little wit
And earn the right to stand or sit,
Hope, love, create, or drink and die:
These shape the creature that is I.[3]

"Long live the weeds." I cannot say that so joyfully as Roethke does. I can acknowledge the ability of weeds to create character in me and thus bring some benefit that I wouldn't otherwise have, but I still wish they weren't here. I still wish upon a star that the world were easier, and that witches could be easily tricked, and dragons slain. I wish there were no suffering. I wish there were no "slaughter of innocents," no Tiny Tims, no Bangladesh, no tyrants, no weeds in this garden.

But weeds exist, so the parable tells us how to live with them. This is not your garden. You just live here. You work here, too. Don't forget that. You do your best. But you are not in charge. That seems to be the hardest lesson for us. You are not in charge. God is. So do your best and leave the rest to God, including judging others.

In the meantime, follow Paul's advice to the Romans. This passage could be Paul's homily on the parable of the wheat and tares. "Live in harmony with one another; do not be haughty, but associate with the lowly; never be conceited. Repay no one evil for evil, but take thought for what is noble in the sight of all. . . . Beloved, never avenge yourselves, but leave it to the wrath of God, for it is written, 'vengeance is mine, I will repay, says the Lord.'. . . Do not be overcome by evil, but overcome evil with good" (Romans 12:16-21).

CHAPTER THREE

The kingdom of heaven is like a mustard seed that someone took and sowed in his field; it is the smallest of all the seeds, but when it has grown it is the greatest of shrubs and becomes a tree, so that the birds of the air come and make nests in its branches.
Matthew 13:31-32

The Mustard Seed

*A*t the beginning of each baseball season, in millions of hearts across this country, there can be heard the expectant cry, "Maybe this will be the year!" There are several lessons about life to be found in the lore of baseball, but none is so prominent and persistent as the analogy of hope.

In April, with the beginning of a new season, everyone gets to start over. The standings at the end of last year are forgotten. Every team starts now with a clean slate, every player begins with a new opportunity. A new season. What a wonderful metaphor of hope. And it comes in the spring, right after Easter, just as nature is being reborn, and when, in church, we are talking about resurrection.

With every new season you hear, "Maybe this will be the year." It can happen, you know, for any team. Even the team that was absolutely terrible last year, deserving of punishment, by grace is given another chance. So this may be the year.

That phrase, "maybe this will be the year," could have come directly out of the Bible. In the Bible everyone is expecting God to act, if not this year, maybe next year. No one really knows when God is going to act, but they have confidence that someday God will act, someday the Kingdom will come, someday the Messiah will be with us.

There are two things about the future of which the Bible is certain: One is that we don't know it; and the second is that God knows it, and therefore God is in charge of all history, including our lives. "But of that day or hour no one knows, not even the angels of heaven, nor the Son, but the Father only" (Matthew 2:36).

According to Jesus, our ignorance of the future should lead to an appropriate humility and the recognition that we are dependent on a power greater than ourselves, who will see to it that there will be a new season, and everyone will have a chance, if not now, then some day. Since we don't know the future, but we know God does, we can have hope that maybe this will be the year.

When Paul says, "We see through a glass darkly," he is describing our inability to see the future. The metaphor asserts that we don't see very well at all. All we have with which to see, Paul says, ". . . are faith, hope and love." According to Paul, the greatest of these is love. According to the parable of the mustard seed, the greatest is "hope."

> *"According to Paul, the greatest of these is love. According to the parable of the mustard seed, the greatest is "hope."*

When Jesus told that parable, the audience got the punch line immediately. Like all punch lines, it comes at the end, the last line. "Birds of the air come and make nests in its branches."

The crowd would have associated that phrase with stories about giant cedars, which were stories about the world's great kingdoms. The cedar was a symbol of political power, so when you heard the phrase, "giant cedars in whose branches birds come and make their nests," you thought of empires.

Jesus' audience undoubtedly thought of Rome, which was occupying the land at the time. Rome was a giant cedar, one of the great kingdoms of all time, in comparison to which the Kingdom of God, as it was then manifest, just a handful of believers, was like a mustard seed, tiny and insignificant, and hidden, buried somewhere in this giant empire, something nobody pays any attention to. Everyone pays attention to the giant cedars, towering over all other life, like the redwoods of California. But no one pays any attention to a bush, or especially the seed of a bush, when it is the smallest seed there is.

Jesus is setting up the punch line. "Birds nest in their branches." In those days when you talked about "kingdoms" you talked about trees, or bushes. Birds nest in trees, not in bushes. Everybody knows that. A tree is a tree, and a bush is a bush, and it will never be any different. It will always be that way. That's called fate, and everybody knows that history is ruled by fate.

Christians do not see history from the perspective of fate, but from the perspective of hope. It is hope that makes the outrageous claim that someday the mustard bush is going to be a tree, even a tree like the Cedars of Lebanon. Hope allows us to understand that the kingdoms of this world will become the Kingdom of our Lord, and the birds will make their nests in its branches.

In the book of Ezekiel it is predicted that one day Israel would be a great cedar, like all the other nations round about her. One day, Ezekiel said, God will take a sprig from the tallest cedar and plant it on the mountain, presumably in Jerusalem. Someday Israel will be like the great nations of the world (Ezekiel 17:22-24).

The radical nature of Jesus' message can be seen in that he doesn't talk about taking a sprig from a cedar. In fact, when he talks about the Kingdom of God, he doesn't talk about a cedar at all, he talks about an unimpressive, lackluster bush, sort of a weed, You've seen the mustard plant. It's unimpressive, which is the way the Kingdom of God looks right now compared to the great empires and institutions of this world. But just wait and see. You never know. In fact, this may be the year.

For the Christian hope is a way of life. It produces at least three qualities, which can be outlined with alliteration: patience, persistence, and perspicacity.

Perspicacity is a word serving to underscore the envisioning power of hope. *Perspicacity* means keenness of vision. It implies a discriminating vision, not fooled by appearances, or attracted to what everybody else notices, but able to see what others can't see. A person with perspicacity evaluates the events of his or her life, or the events of history, with discriminating eyes, a vision that is able to pick out a mustard seed as clearly as a giant cedar.

People with perspicacity rarely use absolutes, such as, "This is the worst thing that could ever happen." They never say, "I don't think I'll get over this," or, "This is the end. We'll never recover from this," or, "I'll never be happy again," or, "He'll always be the same. He'll never change."

Categorical statements about human life, or about history, are the sign of the lack of hope. To believe in God means there will always be possibility. People with perspicacity know that few things can be predicted with absolute certainty, so they always have hope. They have a keenness of vision, a discriminating vision that can see mustard seeds when everybody else can see only the cedars.

One of my past-times is collecting the evidence of predictions gone awry. I found the newest addition in a review of a book entitled *Searching for Certainty: What Scientists Can Know About the Future.* The author concluded that we can know very little about the future, and had an ingenious way of making the point. He evaluated the areas in which scientists often make predictions, giving them letter grades. For instance, he studied predictions on how the stock market will do, or the weather, or when war is going to break out, or how an individual life will turn out. His grades range from B+ for weather prediction to D+ for predicting human behavior. The grade point average for all of the predictions, the GPA for the scientists, was C+.

I say that's not very impressive. These are experts, mind you. We call them experts, anyway. But I would guess that their average is no better than ours if we were predicting the future in those same areas.

In the midst of a drought in California the scientists, using their instruments to measure the weather, said, It's not going to rain again this year. The mayor of San Diego, defying the experts, said, "It's going to rain." They said, "How do you know that?" "I have this feeling," she replied, most unscientifically. They laughed. Everybody laughed. And then it rained. It continued to rain. It rained for a whole month. It was wonderful. She gets the B+; they get the D+.

Perspicacity: It's the keenness of insight that refuses to be taken in by predictions, because it knows who controls the future, and therefore it knows there will always be a new season. So maybe this will be the year.

> "Perspicacity . . . the keenness of insight that refuses to be taken in by predictions."

Which leads to the second characteristic of hope: patience. Patience is the evidence that you know who's in charge, so you can wait for God to act. It's called "waiting on the Lord," and it's the hardest thing for most of us to do. There are some religious people, the Protestant type, for whom it is especially hard. They believe we must always be up and doing. They are always trying to save themselves, or someone else, or the world. None of which we can do. That's

God's business. The hardest thing for us to grasp is that we must let God do that.

Which is why Jesus told so many parables about farmers. In Matthew 13, the parables are literally back-to-back: The Sower, The Wheat and the Tares, The Mustard Seed. One after another. They all say the same thing: be patient. It's as if he wants to hammer it home. Be patient, be patient, be patient. There is only so much that you can do.

That's not a counsel for quietism. We are expected to do something. We are supposed to improve ourselves. We are expected to adopt spiritual disciplines so that we can continue to perfect ourselves. We are supposed to love our neighbors, and be actively involved in doing so, even to the point, when it's appropriate, of intervening to help them. We're expected to make this world a better place, to be active in organizations seeking to do that, and never give up. But we will do all of that better, and without the despair that accompanies the impatient, if we remember there is only so much that we can do. We're like a farmer sowing a seed. That's all we can do. For the rest, we have to wait for God.

Richard Mouw told about the time he was in an ecumenical conference with some Roman Catholics. The question of creation came up. The nuns asked how some conservative Christians could believe in a literal six-day creation. Mouw tried to explain their line of reasoning, although he doesn't share that view himself. When he finished, one of the nuns threw up her hands in exasperation and said, "Don't these people realize that God likes to do things slowly?'

Mouw said it then occurred to him that one reason many conservative Christians have so much difficulty with the questions of racial and economic justice, and bringing peace to this world, is that those problems seem so tenacious, so difficult to solve. They just hang on year after year. So they conclude God must not think these are very important, they must not be on God's agenda, or else God would have done something about them long before now. But God does not act on our time, God acts on God's time. Which is why we should be patient.

And it's also why we should be persistent. That's the third characteristic. Be persistent in good works, because you never know, God may use what you do in a mighty way. You can't control the results of your deeds. God controls that. You could say it's a matter of timing. That's how these things happen, you know. Small deeds become big events when the timing is right. So don't give up. Be persistent.

Hope produces persistence. You don't stop after seven innings if you're behind. You don't stop after seven innings even if you look at what you are up against and it looks like something terrible, some giant cedar, and you feel like a small mustard seed. You don't give up. You keep going clear to the end of the game, because anything can happen. That's the perspective of hope. If God is in charge, anything can happen. So be persistent.

Apparently Horace Walpole once said, "The world is a comedy to those who think, and a tragedy to those who feel." To those who believe, the world is a field in which a seed is planted. It is the smallest of seeds, so it's hard to see. Most people don't even know it's there. They just walk right over it. But it's there. Jesus planted it, and it's growing, slowly, according to God's time.

This parable is here to get you thinking. How will you live in a world in which a kingdom is hidden? How will you live in a world in which most people don't believe it's even here? How will you live in a world for which you pray, "Thy Kingdom come, Thy will be done on earth as it is in heaven"?

One day it's going to happen, in God's time. In the meantime, how will you live?

CHAPTER FOUR

The kingdom of heaven is like treasure hidden in a field, which some-one found and hid; then in his joy he goes and sells all that he has and buys that field. Matthew 13:44-50

The Buried Treasure

I am fascinated with Emily Dickinson. I have interpret-ed her poems in sermons, though with restraint because not everyone is crazy about her. She is diffi-cult to understand, but I find that to be part of the attraction. It's fun to try to figure out what she means.

She has some of the most intriguing metaphors in all poet-ry, and rich in meaning for Christian faith. I save them when I come across them, hold them until some text comes along and claims them. One such is a fascinating poem entitled "Finding Is the First Act." It's perfect for the parables that Jesus told about treasure, and particularly The Parable of the Treasure Buried in the Field.

It is barely a parable. It is only one verse long. "The King-dom of heaven is like treasure hidden in a field, which a man found and covered up; then in his joy he goes and sells all that he has and buys that field" (13:44). You can see in the parable that finding is the first act.

I was familiar with the parable, but that line, "Finding is the first act," from Emily Dickinson, helped me to see it in a different way. Actually, I came across the line, "Finding is the first act," which is quoted in a study of the parables writ-ten by Bernard Scott. He got it from Dominic Crossan, another biblical scholar, who actually wrote a book entitled *Finding Is the First Act.*

I wasn't familiar with the poem, so I looked it up, read it, didn't understand it, which is usually the case for me in reading Emily Dickinson. No problem, I thought. Dominic Crossan uses the line as the title of his book, so surely he will explain it. All I have to do now is get Crossan's book, read it, and find out what the poem meant. I made a note to buy that book.

I was in my office a few days later, went to my bookcase to find another book, and there it was, in my library. I already had Crossan's book. Have you ever had that experience? It's embarrassing, not knowing what you have in your library. I've bought books, saying, "I've got to read this." I read them and say, "I've already read this." I opened Crossan's book, and there were my underlines in the book. I read the book ten years ago, and forgot all about it. So I read it again, and discovered why I had forgotten it. I noticed some of my underlines meandering off the page, a sure sign of dozing off.

I kept reading it, though, the second time, looking for an explanation of Emily Dickinson's poem, "Finding Is the First Act." Surely Crossan is going to say something about this soon. He borrowed the first line of her poem for the title of his book, "Finding Is the First Act." Surely he's going to talk about it some place. I kept digging, It's got to be here somewhere.

Crossan doesn't mention the poem after quoting it in the title. But I don't blame him. After the first line, "Finding is the first act," the poem descends into apparent despair.

> Finding is the first Act
> The second, loss.
> Third, Expedition for
> The "Golden Fleece"
> Fourth, no Discovery—
> Fifth, no Crew—
> Finally, no Golden Fleece—
> Jason-sham-too.[1]

You can hardly preach about that. It's no wonder Crossan doesn't mention the poem after he imitates the opening line. "Borrowing Is the First Act." That is what he should have called his book. I decided that I would follow this example. If reputable scholars can use a line from a poem as a title for their book and not explain it, I can do the same for a sermon title. So I preached the parable once with the title, "Finding Is the First Act." The phrase alone, without the rest of the poem is valuable in unlocking one message of the parable. "The Kingdom of heaven is like treasure hidden in a field which a man found." That seems innocuous enough, except once again Jesus is taking a common story, familiar to everyone, and turning it on its head.

"Borrowing is the First Act"

Treasure stories were common in that culture. Treasure stories are common in every culture. The audience would have been familiar with the story type. The rabbis frequently told treasure parables and the plot was always the same. A man buys a field and works it. His plow hits something hard, and, lo and behold, there's a great teasure, making the man rich.

A classic formula recurs in all treasure stories: first, you buy the field; second, you work hard; and third, you find a treasure. The rabbis wove wonderful stories on the loom of this formula. Here is one. A man buys a field and finds a treasure in his field. He sees two rabbis walking down the road. The rabbis are in tattered clothes, and they are hungry. They haven't eaten for days. Out of compassion the man gives the treasure to the rabbis, goes back to the field, starts plowing, and discovers an even greater treasure.

In the rabbinic version, the message is give and you will get more. That was the common expectation, the orthodox theology, and treasure stories were told to reinforce that theology. The formula is always the same. There is a treasure hidden in the world, which could mean that God is hidden here, or the Kingdom is here someplace, hidden. In other cultures the treasure stories affirmed that salvation, nirvana, your "bliss," or whatever it is you are looking for, is here, hidden in the world. All religions say the same thing. What you are looking for is here, the human venture is to find it, and religion has the map, or the secret, or the clue, or the formula, or the method for finding it.

That's why all religions contain law. The rules are there to lead you to the treasure. Not that it's easy. It is hard obeying the Law. The Law is the Jewish rule for finding the treasure. It's hard work, like plowing a field. If you are persistent, you will find a treasure, but you must follow the formula: First buy the field, then work hard, and then the treasure will be there.

Now look what Jesus does with this: "The Kingdom of heaven is like treasure hidden in a field," (So far, so good) "which a man found, and covered up. Then in his joy he goes and sells all that he has and buys that field."

He is expected to buy the field first, but Jesus says that first he found the treasure; second, he bought the field; third, he didn't work at all. I tell you that this story is an affront to religious piety and to morality. The treasure is supposed to come at the last, the result of some great effort, a long spiritual journey, a tremendous investment of effort, at the least a long, patient waiting.

Treasure stories support what we believe, the way we were raised. Hard work produces reward. You don't get anything in this life without working hard for it. In Aesop's collection of stories there is an illustration of this common wisdom. A farmer had two sons. Both of them were lazy. Neither of them would do any work on the farm. When the farmer was about to die he called his two sons to his bed and said, "I have buried the family treasure in the field." Whereupon his two sons became interested in farming, went to the field and started plowing: (If you want a treasure, you have to work.)

I believe in the work ethic. I was raised that way. Rewards come from hard work. Finding, like dessert, must be last. It should come after a hard day's work, a long, perilous journey, or a patient waiting. But when it comes to the Kingdom, Jesus says, our hard work does not merit rewards. The treasure is hidden.

One of the hardest things for us to grasp is that we are saved by grace and not by our own works. God saved the world because God loved the world, not because the world deserved it, or was particularly lovable. Which means that God doesn't play by the rules, not the rules that we set up. God loved first. You're not supposed to do that. You're supposed to love those who are lovable, who earn your love. You are supposed to forgive those who repent, who are really, sincerely sorry for what they do, and swear that they will never do it again. Then you forgive them.

That's why they couldn't understand Jesus. Jesus didn't say, I'll forgive you when you stop sinning. He said, "I forgive you. Now go and sin no more." The religious professionals couldn't get over the assertion that grace would come to us out of the blue, without our deserving it, without even expecting it.

Jesus said it would be as if you were crossing a field one day. It's not even your field. You're just taking a short-cut across somebody else's field when you stumble upon a treasure that enables you to live the way you have always wanted to live. You can't believe this is happening. You gave up all hope of it ever happening. You assumed that you would never live the life that you were created for, either because of what you had done in the past, or because of what the world had done to you. So after awhile you gave up looking. You no longer expected it to happen.

The message of this parable, in fact the message of the whole New Testament, the message of the Gospel, is that you don't have to find it, because God has found you in Jesus Christ. If we could get that, if it would ever sink into our thick skulls, it would be like finding a treasure without our deserving it, and when we least expect it.

Ironically, the reason we have such difficulty believing is

that we are so religious. I have come to this conclusion. The more religious we are, or perhaps I should say, the more religious our upbringing, the harder it is for us to believe that we are saved by grace and not by our own works. The reason is that religion is so often interpreted as something we are supposed to do, a set of rules we are supposed to follow, the reward of which is salvation.

It is even more difficult to admit that "works-righteousness" is not only a religious problem, it's also the American obsession. If you are a "religious American" you are about as obsessive-compulsive as you get. You will work hard. You will probably work all the time. You're a workaholic. People admire you for that. "Old Joe, he was a hard worker. You've got to admire him. Of course, he was a bore, but he was a hard worker. Right up to the moment he croaked, he was a hard worker. He went the way he wanted to, working hard."

> *"If you are a "religious American" you are about as obsessive-compulsive as you get."*

Do you know such persons? Something is wrong, sort of a malaise. They can't put their finger on it, they don't know what it is. They come to me sometimes, as they come to all pastors. I ask them "Things going all right? The job, the family, the kids?" "Everything is fine." And I'm sure it is because I know this person. They are successful, they have wealth enough to live comfortably. They have status, they are respected in their profession and in their town. And they have security. Their future is taken care of. Everything is all right . . . except something is wrong.

It's remarkably the same, whether they be young or old, Catholic or Protestant, male or female. A home where love was a reward for good behavior, and where the lessons learned were lessons on how to be successful through competition, and where, no matter how hard you worked, no matter how successful you were, it was never quite enough. "You did very well on this, but you should have done it this way. It could have been a little better."

Religious communities support these obsessions. Even if the person has had a conversion experience, either early or late in life, the basic orientation, the idea that life is something to be earned, doesn't really change. Conversion, in other words, doesn't convert, it eases the pressure, gives them some relief from guilt for not being somebody else. After which they go right back to the business of trying to be that somebody else.

So many people live as if they have to justify their existence, as if they have to offer proof that they are worth something. They would understand Paul's diagnosis of our condition. He used the word "justify," a legal term, because in his culture life was measured against the law. He said nothing we can do will justify our lives when held up to the complexity of the Law. By grace God has considered us as just through the cross of Christ. If you are punishing yourself, or depriving yourself, because you feel you don't measure up to some "Law," some standard of perfection, the good news is that God in Christ considers you to be just even though you have difficulty seeing yourself that way.

That message was so contrary to common wisdom and religious counsel both then and now, that the good people were offended by it. Jesus was offering grace, and said that's what you are really looking for. Besides, it's right here in front of you. "I have come that you might have life." I am offering it to you as a gift. Finding the treasure is the first act, not the last. We are saved by grace, not our works.

Maybe Emily Dickinson's poem, written in the post-Puritan early nineteenth century, and, in those days, one of the most uptight regions of our country, western Massachusetts, is about the difficulty of trusting grace. Can it be interpreted that way? It may not be her intent, but then again, it may be.

And besides, who will know? Old Emily has been gone a long time.

> Finding is the first Act
> The second, loss,
> Third, Expedition for
> The "Golden Fleece"
> Fourth, no Discovery
> Fifth, no Cre—
> Finally, no Golden Fleece—
> Jason-Sham-too.

The story of Jason and the Golden Fleece is a treasure story, one of the oldest treasure stories, out of Greek mythology. Jason is tricked out of the kingdom that is rightfully his by inheritance. In order to get it back, he must go on a journey, suffer many hardships, sail across perilous seas, face many dangers. In the end, with the help of Medea, he succeeds in winning his kingdom back and lives the way he was supposed to live, as royalty.

Emily Dickinson's poem is about the difficulty of trusting grace. We know that she wrestled with grace all of her life. She wrote, "We both believe and disbelieve A hundred times an hour." It's as if one day she discovered grace, just stumbled on it: "Finding is the first act." But then disbelieved: "The second, loss." Then went on a search to recover it: "The third, expedition for the Golden Fleece."

She "believed and disbelieved" because it is so hard to trust that God loves us the way we are. It is so hard for us to believe that God loves us when we have been taught that we have to earn love. It is so hard to trust that God is offering us new life as a gift when we have been taught that we must deserve life. So, we conclude, this can't be for us, this promise. Maybe it is for those who are so dramatically lost that all they can do is reach for some rope to pull them up. Maybe it is for them. It is not for me. I keep trying.

So like Jason, we go looking for the kingdom that we know is ours. We know it is here someplace. It is an expedition for the Golden Fleece, for the life we hope will be better than the life we live now. We look, therefore, for all kinds of things in all kinds of places, but what we're really looking for has already been offered to us as grace.

We find grace, but we don't believe it, so we end up imitating Jason rather than Jesus, looking for the Golden Fleece, or the golden opportunity, or the gold at the end of the rainbow. And then eventually, some day, we discover they are sham, and Jason too.

It was to these people Jesus said, what you are looking for is like a treasure hidden in a field. A man stumbled over it, fell right on his face. This had happened to him before. Each time he got up, dusted off his clothes, cursed his clumsiness, and continued the search. But this time he said, maybe this is it. Maybe this is what I've been looking for. And so he began to dig into the Gospel promise of grace and discovered that God found him first.

CHAPTER FIVE

> *Take care that you do not despise one of these little ones; for, I tell you,*
> *in heaven their angels continually see the face of my Father in heaven.*
> *What do you think? If a shepherd has a hundred sheep, and one of*
> *them has gone astray, does he not leave the ninety-nine on the moun-*
> *tains and go in search of the one that went astray? And if he finds it,*
> *truly I tell you, he rejoices over it more than over the ninety-nine that*
> *never went astray. So it is not the will of your Father in heaven that*
> *one of these little ones should be lost.*
> *Matthew 18:10-14*

The Lost Sheep

If you read the eighteenth chaper of Matthew, the setting for The Parable of the Lost Sheep, you will conclude that someone is in trouble. This person may have done something against the strict rules of the Church, either in doctrine or in morals. Those rules were important and not to be taken lightly. The Church was in the world to redeem the world, to hold up a better way of living. To that end, persons renounced the world when they became Christian, which didn't mean they withdrew into some separate, monastic existence. It simply meant that when it came to behavior Christians were to ask, what would Jesus do, not what does the crowd do.

The temptation to be like the world was always there. That's why they prayed, "Lead us not into temptation." They prayed that every day. We pray that, too, though for most of us temptation is not that big a thing. I recall the man who said, "I found a way to get rid of temptation. Yield to it." I know many people like that. In fact, that attitude pretty much dominates our age. In our time, temptation is a joke. In our time, "The Temptations" is a singing group from Detroit. Temptation has been trivialized because the tension between the Christian life and the life of the world is nearly gone. It's sagging because we have yielded to the world, becoming like the world, even using the Church to bless the way the world does things. Many people, in fact, think that the Church exists to bless the world, not to change the world.

In baptism and in the renewal of baptism we "renounce the spiritual forces of wickedness, the evil powers of this world, and repent of our sins." What does that mean? Most of us have no idea what it means. The language of the baptism vow provokes us to think about the way the world operates, the way it gets things done. It prompts us as Christians to ask, "Can I do that? Where do I draw the line"? What do I renounce when I become a Christian?

At Matthew's church they knew the answer immediately. They knew what Christians shouldn't do, and evidently some guy did it. So they kicked him out. They didn't horse around in those days. There was no pussyfooting in the Church. If you didn't live up to the standards of the community you were out.

The Methodists started that way two hundred years ago when they were a reform movement within the Church of England. It continued to be the practice a while after they became a Church in America. In those days you were assigned small groups called class meetings, and you were accountable for your behavior within those class meetings. If your behavior wasn't exemplary, the class leader could expel you.

It's a little different now. Now they say that the United Methodist Church is the easiest church to get into and the hardest church to get out of. But it wasn't always that way, and certainly not that way in Matthew's church. It was very hard to get in, and if you didn't live up to your vows, you were out.

> *"It was very hard to get in, and if you didn't live up to your vows, you were out."*

Matthew is interpreting The Parable of the Lost Sheep for his church. Here's the situation. Somebody has been kicked out of the Church for what they have done. Or maybe they know they are going to be kicked out, so they're staying away. In other words, Matthew says, "Go get him. Bring him back, forgive him, and restore him to the fellowship."

There is no question that Matthew wants us to go after that person. Don't let her dangle out there. Don't let him suffer. He argues it with force. The whole eighteenth chaper is one long argument for forgiveness. He begins with Jesus' teaching about humility, illustrated with Jesus placing a little child in the midst of the disciples and saying, "This is what I mean by humility" (18:1-6).

Have you ever known a little child to hold a grudge? I was amazed many times, watching my children grow up, that they could dry their tears and start playing again with those with whom they had just been arguing and fighting. Sometimes it took a little intervention and persuasion, but they didn't have trouble doing it. Have you ever noticed this? Children are not interested in making people pay for their sins. They forgive easily. They have to be taught that the adult way to deal with these things is to pout, and be offended, and stretch it out as long as you can, to make the very most of it.

Years ago I counseled a couple. The man came to repentance. I said to the woman. "Now will you forgive him?" "No," she said. "Why not?" I asked. "He hasn't suffered enough," she said. That's the way adults do it. Jesus put a child in their midst, and said, Can you imagine a child doing that? Be like a child.

Next Matthew puts in a word about temptation, just to show, I guess, that he's not soft on sin (18:7-9). Then an admonition from the Lord, "See that you do not despise one of these little ones," (18:10) as a transition to the very heart of the chapter, The Parable of the Lost Sheep, about a shepherd who leaves the ninety-nine and goes after the one who is lost.

After the parable he fires a few more volleys. First, advice on how to handle disputes in church (18:15-20). Then Peter's question, "How many times shall my brother sin against me and I forgive him?" The answer: "Seventy times seven," which is another way of saying, "Without end" (18:21-22). He concludes the chapter with another parable about a servant who was forgiven by his master but who wouldn't forgive his fellow servant (18:23-35).

Matthew arranges the material to make a strong case for forgiveness in a church where someone is in trouble. They have disciplined him, ostracized him, probably excommunicated him. The message is here for that kind of church, and for those who deal with anyone that way: Righteousness accompanied by censoriousness is not Christian. Righteousness, in order to be Christian, must be accompanied by forgiveness.

> *"Righteousness accompanied by censoriousness is not Christian."*

That's the way Matthew uses this parable, to talk about forgiveness. But I wonder if Jesus told it with a different emphasis, a different twist. Listen to it again.

A shepherd leaves the ninety-nine sheep and goes after the one that is lost. Which means that this parable is about a leader who abandons those who behave themselves, who play by the rules, never stray from the straight and narrow, never get into trouble, and gives his attention to the one who breaks the rules, gets caught, and has to be bailed out.

Which makes it similar to the parable where a father had two sons. One stayed home and was obedient to the father, the other took his inheritance and went away into a far country and wasted it on riotous living. One day the second son came home. The father left the righteous son and embraced the one who was lost (Luke 15:11-21).

This parable is for anyone who thinks that God belongs to those who have been good to God. Jesus ran into such ideas when he came preaching about those who believe that God is on our side, and that righteousness has its privileges—God will obviously endorse, bless, preserve, and prosper all of our endeavors. It makes sense that God would like us better than them. It makes sense that God would rather be with us than with them. Don't you agree?

I saw the movie *Romero* some years ago about the martyred bishop of El Salvador, but I rented it and watched it again in the light of this parable. (It would have been a better movie with fewer straw men. The good guys are just too good, the bad guys are too bad.) It's a compelling story of a Christian who undergoes a transformation when he sees the relevance of Jesus' teachings to the world in which he lives. When he does that, he discovers there are some things he must renounce if he is to remain Christian.

He was made bishop, according to the script, because prior to that time he had no discernible views. Evidently it was considered a great advantage for a bishop to be innocuous. But sometimes something happens after you are ordained. You begin to live into, or up to your office, your calling. A bishop is ordained to be a shepherd. He carries a shepherd's crook. He is the shepherd of the flock. That's the definition of a bishop. To whom should the shepherd give his attention. With whom should the shepherd stand in the conflict in El Salvador?

The story of Archbishop Romero is the story of a shepherd

leaving the ninety and nine, the established Church, the respectable people, and going to the lost. That's why they killed him. While he was celebrating mass on the steps of the Cathedral in San Salvador they shot him, because he went after the lost sheep.

There is a scene in the movie where a woman of the wealthy ruling class comes to the bishop, who is her friend, and says, "Now is the time for you to baptize my baby."

He says, "I will be happy to do it. We'll do it on the second Sunday in December."

"You will, of course, do it privately."

"No, I will do it in the church on Sunday."

The woman, knowing that on Sunday the church is filled with the poor says, "I will not have my baby baptized with Indians."

Do you see the question? Whose side is God on? Jesus was in trouble from the very beginning because those to whom he went, with whom he sided, and to whom he ministered, were considered "lost" by the establishment. Of course, he said that God doesn't take sides. God sends the rain on the just and the unjust. God is impartial, God doesn't take sides—not until one of God's children, or races, or classes of oppressed or forgotten are in any way excluded from the family of God, especially by those who say, "We are the family of God." That's when God takes sides, and there is no question at all about which side God is on.

Would God leave the righteous, God's own people, those who have been loyal to God for centuries, to be with those that we wouldn't associate with? The answer in the New Testament is unequivocally "yes." The gospels vary only in the many ways they say "yes." In this text it is being said with a parable about the lost sheep.

A great history is evident in the title *shepherd*. We read it in the Old Testament, particularly in Ezekiel. There the leaders of the nation are called shepherds (Ezekiel 34;1-6). The kings are the shepherds, after King David, the first shepherd king.

It's also a description of their vocation. The kings, the leaders of the people, are expected to care for all the people. Ezekiel says the kings are not doing that, therefore God himself will come to be the shepherd and gather up all the people (Ezekiel 34:11-16).

Jesus says, I am that shepherd. What I am doing is exactly what Ezekiel prophesied. If someone is in need, God doesn't look at their passport. God doesn't look at their baptismal certificate. God doesn't even look at their past, but like a shepherd, or like a parent, God drops everything and goes to them.

Would you leave us to be with them? "Watch me," Jesus said. And he ate with sinners; he spent the night in the house of a tax collector; he praised a Centurion, who was the enemy; he touched the untouchables to heal them; he forgave people he had no business forgiving. A shepherd goes to those who are lost.

In the Gospel of John Jesus says it out loud, "I am the good shepherd" (John 10:11). It's so comforting. The shepherd knows the sheep. The shepherd knows the sheep so well that he knows their names. Jesus knows all of our names. It's so comforting, so intimate, so exclusive, until he says, "I have sheep who are not of this flock." Who could they be? Could they be the ones that Matthew is talking about—the lost? Where do you think the shepherd is? Where do you think our leader is? Has anyone seen the shepherd?

Matthew ends the teaching section of the Gospel with a parable called The Parable of the Last Judgment. This comes at the end of Matthew 25. The Gospel is divided into a teaching section and a passion section, the passion referring to the Cross. The teaching section concludes with The Parable of the Last Judgment, after which Jesus heads immediately for Jerusalem. So the story of the Last Judgment *is* his last word, a summary statement.

It's about a shepherd who, at the end of the day, separates the sheep from the goats. The sheep go to the right, the goats go to the left. We all started as sheep. Along the way, some of us turned into old goats. The goats say, How come I can't get into the Kingdom? What did I do? The shepherd says, That's the very point. You didn't do anything. "I was in prison, you didn't visit me. I was hungry, you didn't feed me. I was naked, you didn't give me any blankets. I was sick, you didn't come to me." "When were you that way? We never saw you that way. The only people we know that way are, you know, 'them.' And they are not of this flock." The shepherd says, "If you have done it unto the least of these you have done it to me."

We must take Matthew as a whole. Start at the beginning: read all the way through. When you do, you can see that the end helps interpret what goes before. The Parable of the Judgment throws light on The Parable of the Lost Sheep.

If you read The Lost Sheep in light of The Last Judgment, here is what it says: When the shepherd goes after the one who is lost, the ninety-nine are expected to follow him.

Or you can put it as a question. If the leader is with the one, and the ninety-nine refuse to follow, then who is lost?

CHAPTER SIX

> When evening came, the owner of the vineyard said to his manager,
> "Call the laborers and give them their pay, beginning with the last
> and then going to the first." When those hired about five o'clock
> came, each of them received the usual daily wage. Now when the
> first came, they thought they would receive more; but each of them
> also received the usual daily wage. And when they received it, they
> grumbled against the landowner, saying "These last worked only one
> hour, and you have made them equal to us who have borne the bur-
> den of the day and the scorching heat." But he replied to one of them,
> "Friend I am doing you no wrong; did you not agree with me for the
> usual daily wage? Take what belongs to you and go; I choose to give
> to this last the same as I give to you. Am I not allowed to do what I
> choose with what belongs to me? Or are you envious because I am
> generous?" So the last will be first, and the first will be last.
> Matthew 20:1-16

The Laborers in the Vineyard

The Parable of The Laborers in the Vineyard is about a landowner who hires laborers at different times of the day but pays them all the same wage. It seems patently unfair. Those who work longer, those who have seniority, ought to get more pay. But they all get the same wage, those who were hired early in the morning, and those who were hired at the "eleventh hour." A situation guaranteed to result in the filing of a labor grievance, which is exactly what happens. "They grumbled against the landholder." The landowner replied, "Am I not allowed to do what I choose with what belongs to me? Take what belongs to you and go."

Then comes one of those profound sayings that Jesus likes to throw in at the conclusion of his parables. "The first shall be last, and the last shall be first," which sounds as arbitrary as the boss saying, "I can do what I want with what is mine." It's an unassailable statement, unchallengeable. It's absolutely accurate. But is it fair?

The landowner says he is being generous, giving a denarius for a day's work, therefore they have no right to complain. That's what they contracted for. He says, "I am being generous giving that to you." But that could be challenged. In the first place, a denarius was no big deal. It was, in fact, a typical day's wage for that kind of work. And besides, one could argue that it's up to the recipient, not the donor, to define generosity.

Is the point of the parable, "Keep working and stop your griping?" Or does it say something else to us? We've looked at enough parables in Matthew by now to know that if you take a few steps backwards and examine them from some distance, you may get a different perspective. That's because the parables in Matthew are not isolated anecdotes, but part of a larger context and often used as the conclusion of a point, or an argument, that Matthew is making.

When we step back from the parable, moving back to the beginning of Matthew 19, we are in the midst of a dispute between Jesus and the Pharisees about marriage and divorce.

The Pharisees begin by pointing out that Moses allowed for divorce. Jesus counters with the argument from Genesis, the story of creation, where it says, "God created them male and female." That's the basis for marriage, according to Jesus. Marriage is grounded in creation, which is to say, marriage is the way God intended things to be. "For this reason a man shall leave his father and mother and be joined to his wife, and the two shall become one flesh" (19:5). A wonderful image. It says to mothers and fathers, who don't want to let go of their children, that this bewildering phenomenon is part of creation. God intended that we should leave mother and father and be joined with someone else. "And the two shall become one flesh." "Male and female he created them."

Jesus based this remark on one of the two creation stories in Genesis, the one in the first chapter. There's also a story of creation in the second chapter, which says the same thing, but in a different and much more poetic way. After Adam is created God said, "It is not right that he should be alone," which means that the first thing that God declared "not good" is loneliness. So he created Eve from Adam's rib, meaning male and female are really one flesh, which explains the mysterious and irresistible attraction: They are made for each other.

That's why Jesus says to parents, you'd better get ready, because one of these days your son or your daughter is going to leave and be joined to someone else, and the two will try to become one flesh. Then he throws in another of his profound sayings. This saying is in the traditional wedding ceremony. "Therefore what God has joined together, let no one put asunder."

According to this view, marriage is a means of approximating the Garden of Eden, life the way God intended. Marriage should be structured to allow two people to become one flesh, which is why it must be monogamous, exclusive, and for a lifetime. It takes a long, long time, and much work, for two people to become one flesh. David Mazel writes about his grandmother, who is talking about her marriage. "The years go by and we get more alike, your grandfather and I. Sometimes we have the same thought at the same time. The thought just shines in our two heads. Who knows, one day we may not even need to speak, we may just wave at each other from time to time, like old friends climbing a mountain together."

To become one flesh in marriage is a task that takes many years. Thus divorce is not part of God's plan. Jesus pauses. The Pharisees say, "But what about Moses? Who are you to contradict Moses, the giver of the Law, who allowed for divorce?" Jesus' answer is critical, not only for the understanding of the issue of marriage and divorce, but also for all that follows in this chapter, including The Parable of the Laborers in the Vineyard. What about Moses? He allowed divorce, and Moses spoke for God. So it must be God's will. Jesus replies that Moses allowed divorce because of the "the hardness of your hearts" (19:8).

He must have said that with some sadness, the same sadness with which he wept over Jerusalem when he said, "Jerusalem, Jerusalem! Would I have gathered you as a hen gathers her brood under her wings, but you would not." The mothering image reveals that God intends that we would receive God's love and live as one family. "Would I have gathered you . . . but you would not . . . because of the hardness of your hearts.

Because of that hardening, there will be tragedy in life, and pain, and bitterness, and division. Instead of one flesh there will be separation and loneliness. Instead of one community among all people in this world, there will be alienation, and suspicion, and enmity. All because of the hardening of the heart.

Because of the hardening of the heart, life will be hard, not only in the sense of being difficult, but hard in the sense of being unyielding, impenetrable, metallic, uncaring, unfeeling, impersonal. For that reason life must be ordered by rules, and laws, and judgments and contracts, the things that protect you from others who would take advantage of you. That's the kind of world we inhabit. When hearts are hardened, you must look out for yourself.

> *"Life will be hard . . . in the sense of being unyielding, impenetrable, metallic, uncaring, unfeeling, impersonal."*

Hardening of the heart is another term for sin, and a good metaphor for it. Sin has made the world hard and unyielding, uncaring and rigid. The world is defined by orthodoxies and rules, ideologies, creeds, and philosophies that divide people one from another. Races and nations build walls between themselves and others, hard walls, walls of mortar and stone. Separation and segregation depersonalize, and once you depersonalize the other person, it is easier to manipulate them, even destroy them. It is why we can tolerate the killing of thousands in war, even cheering when hearing the news. There is only one way to explain that; our hearts have hardened.

The parable presupposes that who we are now is not who we should be. When we are, there will be no laws; there will be only community. There will be no need for justice, nor will there be need to assert our rights. There will be only community where we live as God intended us to live in the creation, as one flesh, or one body.

I would like to think that our homes and churches are two places where life can exist the way God created it to be, where love can build genuine community so that there is no need for laws to insure that people are protected from the harm that others will do them. It is possible in home, and in church, and in other communities, to come close to the way that God intends. Some of us are blessed to have been raised in such homes. Some of us have been redeemed in such churches.

From the beginning the Church understood that it should be that kind of community. You can see it in a scene from the Acts of the Apostles, the story of the beginning of the Church. In Peter's sermon at Pentecost he says, "Save yourselves from this crooked generation" (Acts 2:40). In other words, be different from the way the world organizes its life. "Save yourselves from this crooked generation."

The world organizes its life according to the hardness of our hearts. But the mission of the Church is to create a new community where people can see the way things are supposed to be. And "all who believed were together and had all things in common; and they sold their possessions and goods and distributed them to all, as any had need. And day by day, attending the Temple together and breaking bread in their homes, they partook of food with glad and generous hearts" (Acts 2:44-47). "Glad and generous hearts" instead of "hardened hearts." A new way of living in this world is based on "glad and generous hearts" not on rules, nor on laws, based not even on our rights, nor on territory, on property, on treaties, nor on any kind of contract—because of what God has done for us in Jesus Christ. Rules and contracts won't work when the concern is not to protect myself but to give myself, and relationships are defined not by justice but by generosity.

> *"Glad and generous hearts" instead of "hardened hearts."*

Having looked at the message of The Parable of the Laborers from a distance, we can understand it better. It's about life in the Kingdom, or life in the Church, or wherever people have the courage to establish the Kingdom.

In the Kingdom there will be a new rule. Better yet, in the Kingdom there will be only one rule: God will be in charge. In the Kingdom life will be the way God intends it to be. Which is why the householder says, "Friend, I am doing you no wrong. . . . Am I not allowed to do what I choose with what belongs to me?" (20:13).

The parable starts out with a landowner and employees, but it ends up looking more like a parent with a family, because that's the best human analogy for the Kingdom—the family. And the best human analogy for God is the parent.

Most commonly we use the analogy of the father for God.

That has become the traditional way of thinking about God. But sometimes mother is a better way. Mothers deal with us according to rules, too. Sometimes mothers have to lay down the law. But at other times, at certain critical times, they act not according to what we have done or what we have earned, but in response to something deep inside of themselves. We ask, Why did you do that? It wasn't fair to the others? They probably wouldn't have a rational reason, if asked. Nor could they point to some rule and justify it on that basis. They just seemed to know it was the right thing to do, and the right time to do it.

A woman being interviewed on television was one of those heroic mothers who raised a large family single-handedly. She not only raised them, but they were all successful, each having made remarkable achievements in his or her vocation. It was a wonderful story, worth celebrating. You've heard it, because it's common. You hear it all the time. And it's worth celebrating, because even though it's common, it's hard, and it takes a lot of sacrifice.

In an attempt to get at some formula, some rule that others could apply in order to have similar success with their families, the mother was asked, "I suppose you loved all your children equally, making sure they all got the same treatment?"

The mother replied, "I loved them. I loved them all, each one of them, but not equally. I loved the one that was down until he was up. I loved the one that was weak until she was strong. I loved the one that was hurt until he was healed. I loved the one that was lost until she was found."[2]

The Kingdom of God is like a mother who loves all her children according to their need, and loves them until they become who they were created to be. It's like that, where rules, and laws, and handing out rewards according to behavior are sometimes put aside, and for some reason deep in the mother's heart, unknown and unexplained to us, she, for a season, puts the first last and the last first. If we can't understand that, it is because of the hardness of our hearts.

Or it's like a landowner who hired workers in the vineyard. He hired all kinds of people and paid them all the same wage. Some who were there didn't understand such grace, and so they complained bitterly, because of the hardness of their hearts. "And the landowner said, 'Am I now allowed to do what I choose with what belongs to me? Or do you begrudge my generosity?' So the last will be first, and the first last."

CHAPTER SEVEN

> *But when the king came in to see the guests, he noticed a man there who was no wearing a wedding robe, and he said to him, 'Friend, how did you get in here without a wedding robe?'" And he was speechless. Then the king said to the attendants, "Bind him hand and foot, and throw him into the outer darkness, where there will be weeping and gnashing of teeth." For many are called, but few are chosen.*
> *Matthew 22:1-14*

The Wedding Banquet

Recently my wife and I were in a restaurant in New York where men are required to wear a tie. You can tell it wasn't a restaurant in San Diego. In San Diego you know that you are in a high class restaurant when they require you to wear shoes. But this was a New York restaurant. Some man came in without a tie. No problem. The maitre d' reached into a drawer and gave him a tie.

In the Parable of the Wedding Banquet, some poor bloke shows up at the banquet without a wedding garment and as a result he gets bound hand and foot and thrown into the outer darkness. Why couldn't the maitre d' just reach into a drawer and give him a wedding garment? Surely there were some extra ones around the palace.

Besides, the fellow was off the street. Some servant, sent out to make the announcement, handed him a bill that said, "If you want to attend the wedding banquet in honor of the kings son, just come." So he came as he was, and the king blew him away. That seems excessive to me, overreactive, and most unlike Jesus, who is telling this parable.

So I was curious. What's got into Jesus? When confused,

read the context. That's always good advice, read the context. Immediately before The parable of the marriage feast is the parable of the vineyard. Maybe there is help there.

The parable of the vineyard (Matthew 21:33-41) is about an owner who lets out his vineyard to some tenants. The time for the harvest comes, the owner sends servants to fetch the grapes. The tenants beat up the servants. He sends some more servants. The tenants beat up those servants, even killing some. So he sends his son, saying, "They will respect my son." But they kill his son, too, thinking maybe they can get his inheritance. "Now, when the owner of the vineyard comes," Jesus asks, "what will he do to those tenants?" They said to him, "He will put those wretches to a miserable death, and lease the vineyard to other tenants who will give him the produce at the harvest time."

Before the parable of the vineyard is the parable of the two sons (Matthew 21:28-31), one who said he would go and work and didn't, and the other who said he would not go, but ended up going. Which one did the will of the Father, the one who talks or the one who does something?

Keep reading the context. Jesus gets in an argument with the priests in the Temple about authority (Matthew 21:23-28), and before that there is the scene called "the cursing of the fig tree" (Matthew 21:18-22). Aha! We may have found something. Jesus was walking down the road with his disciples early in the morning. He saw a fig tree with no fruit on it. He cursed it. The tree withered, right before their eyes. I think we have a clue here. We are finally to the bottom of it. It was a bad day.

> ## "The tree withered, right before their eyes. . . . It was a bad day."

The day began with Jesus zapping a fig tree, revealing what kind of a mood he was in. Maybe it was just one of those days. You know it's going to be one of those days when you are walking along the road with the Master, he spies a fig tree and zaps it, disintegrates it, right before your eyes, leaving a little spiral of smoke coming up from a pile of ashes by the roadside. If I were walking with him on that morning, I think I'd look out. It's going to be one of those days. If the boss, upon arriving at the office, kicked over the water cooler and cursed, I think I'd stay in my office the rest of that day, or maybe go home. You know it's going to be one of those days. Evidently it was.

He cursed the tree on the way to Jerusalem. When he arrived at the Temple he got into a shouting match with the priests and the elders of the Temple over authority. Jesus turned his back on them, refused to answer their questions, and walked away.

Then come the three parables. The Parable of the Two Sons is simple enough. A classic parable. But the next two are something different. In fact, perhaps reflecting his mood, he's changed them from parables to allegories. In an allegory everything in the story generally represents something or someone outside of the story. A parable has some ambiguity. It leaves room for interpretation. In an allegory there is less latitude, so there is less question about whom Jesus is talking. The Parable of the Vineyard is about an owner's son who is rejected and killed by those who don't respect the owner, and what will happen to them. They will be killed, and the ranch will be given to those who will produce fruit.

The Parable of the Wedding Feast is also an allegory. It's about a king who gives a wedding banquet for his son, a reference to the time of the Messiah which was prophesied to be like a marriage banquet. The king sends an invitation to all the right people. The ones he has known for years. His people. The ones he has chosen as his friends. But they say no. They turn down a king! When a king gives an invitation, you are supposed to say "yes." But these people say "no" and deliver a series of lame excuses. so the king sent troops and murdered those people and burned their city, a reference to the destruction of Jerusalem. The king then invited others, strangers, "both the good and the bad." That means everybody is invited. So the wedding hall was filled with guests.

Now in comes this poor guy without a wedding garment. He gets bound hand and foot, and thrown into the outer darkness. The parable ends with this saying: "Many are called but few are chosen." Given what happened to this guest, I don't think I would like to be one of those called.

This procession of hard sayings and vindictive allegories through Matthew 21 and 22 makes you think it must have been a bad day. Jesus started off on the wrong foot. We know what that's like. He began cursing a fig tree because it bore no fruit, and ended by telling a parable about a man who is cursed because he has no wedding garment. It was a frustrating day.

But maybe the fig tree incident gives us a clue to what follows. The fig tree obviously has to do with bearing fruit. "And seeing a fig tree by the side of the road, he went to it and found nothing at all on it, but leaves" (Matthew 21:19). Everything that happens on that day, as a matter of fact, has to do with that theme of bearing fruit. And we know what bearing fruit means. Bearing fruit means living out your faith in your daily lives. It means loving your neighbor. Jesus makes that abundantly clear. Being Christian means that you are to bear fruit.

Who are his disciples? "By these fruits you shall know them."

Which son did the will of the father? The one who bore fruit.

Who gets the vineyard? The ones who give the owner "the produce at the harvest time."

Who gets into the banquet? The one with the wedding garment.

Wearing the wedding garment is something like bearing fruit. To wear a wedding garment to the banquet is to know what kind of event this is. It's to know who is being honored here. To wear a wedding garment is to know how to honor the Son of God.

> ## *"Wearing the wedding garment is something like bearing fruit."*

Jesus is talking about the Kingdom, the reign of God, the coming age, when the Son of God will finally come in his glory. That event will be like a banquet. "On this mountain, the Lord of hosts will make for all peoples a feast of rich food" (Isaiah 25:6-9).

That's what this parable is about. It's about the Kingdom banquet and what it will be like. There will be a judgment, the criterion for which will be, did you bear fruit? "Did you do it to the least of these, my brethren?" Did you live a life worthy of your calling? Are you coming to the wedding feast dressed appropriately?

In looking at the Parable of the Lost Sheep, we suggested that perhaps Matthew was writing to a church that was too judgmental, and so he was giving them instructions about forgiveness. In this parable it sounds like he's addressing a church that is "wallowing in grace," as Fred Craddock puts it, enjoying the love that God has given to us, accepting all things, "I'm OK, You're OK." Not making any demands on anybody. Not considering that "to whom much is given, much is required." Not considering that "many are called, but few are chosen." This parable reminds us that grace is for everyone. Grace is free. It's for everyone. But something is expected from those who receive grace. Fruit is expected. Good works. The ability to come to the banquet dressed appropriately.

Jan Karski was born in Poland, and now is a citizen of this country. He teaches at Georgetown University. Elie Wiesel found him there, living in obscurity, trying to keep out of sight. Wiesel, as you may know, studies the Holocaust, and won the Nobel Prize for raising our consciousness about the significance of that event. He came across the name of Jan Karski in his studies of the Holocaust and discovered that Karski had written a book about the Holocaust in 1944.

Karski was a courier for the Polish underground, and the Polish government in exile from the years 1939 to 1942. He was captured by, and escaped from, both the Gestapo and the Soviets. He was given the assignment to return to Poland, to the Warsaw Ghetto, and to that notorious concentration camp, Belzec, to see if the rumors about the Jews were true.

He reported that the worst was true, and took on the mission of informing the leaders of the Allied nations of what was happening. That brought him to America and President Roosevelt. Roosevelt listened without comment. He talked to Justice Frankfurter, who was a Jew, and who said he didn't believe him. He then gave some lectures around the country, wrote that book in 1944, and then dropped out of sight until Wiesel found him.

Wiesel told Claude Lanzmann, who made that epic TV documentary called *Shoah*, about this Pole living in America who was witness to the Holocaust. When Lanzmann interviewed Karski for that film, bringing him out of obscurity, Karski decided to tell his story. When asked why, after all of those years of being silent, had he decided to speak again, he said there were two reasons. First, because a whole generation has grown up not knowing what happened, not knowing what race prejudice and hatred toward other people can do if it's not opposed. Secondly, he said, "I did it because I believe there will be last judgment, and God will say to me, 'Karski, I gave you a soul. Your body is gone, but your soul is mine. I gave it to you. What did you do with your soul?' And I will have to answer him."[1]

Your soul is like the wedding garment. It's your soul that you take to the banquet. Your soul is what you are to wear into the Kingdom. That's why the maitre d' can't reach down into some drawer and give you your soul. You were given one when you were created, and you were to take care of it, not lose it, so that you will have something to wear, the proper attire at the wedding banquet of the Son. That's why Jesus said, "What good does it do you to gain the whole world and lose your soul?"

Which brings us to another detail in this parable or allegory. Who are these people who turned down the invitation? If this was originally an allegory, and not Matthew's redaction, then these people are undoubtedly the Jews who said "No" to Jesus as the Messiah. That was a terrible sorrow for the early Christians. All the early Christians were Jews. They could not understand why their brothers and sisters did not see what they saw. It was a mystery to them. They didn't understand it. The New Testament is filled with the record of their preoccupation with the rejection of Jesus as the Messiah, some of which has unfortunately been used as a source of anti-Semitism, even in our day.

Anti-Semitism is a sin. Anti-Semitism is an evil, as the wholesale condemnation of any race or group of people is an evil. And what is more, it is unwarranted by an honest and a faithful reading of these passages. They are not to be read as descriptions of somebody else, somebody who lived back there 2,000 years ago. To read scripture faithfully is to ask, does this describe me? Is Jesus talking about me?

The parable is talking about anyone who is in danger of losing their soul because they are so preoccupied with saving themselves, gaining the things of this world, that they say they don't have time for grace. It is about those who would sell the garment that they are supposed to wear to the banquet in order to buy more things now. It's about those who pursue security in this world, rather than service to this world.

Flannery O'Connor in her novel *Wise Blood*, has the preacher say, "Nobody with a good car needs to be justified."[2] That's a North American creed. We're fascinated with these machines. Most North Americans, when they get a new car, sing the *Nunc Dimittis*, "Lord, now lettest thou thy servant depart in peace, for mine eyes have seen thy salvation." It's right here, on four wheels. They don't need grace. They've got all they need right now. Most North Americans, I would say, believe the secular religion promulgated by advertising, which proclaims that I am able to make it by myself. I don't need grace, all I need is the right car, the right something. All I need is something to possess, to accumulate, and my soul will be satisfied.

The parable is not here to point the finger at somebody who lived two thousand years ago; it is here to ask you, are you in that group who, to the invitation of grace, said no, because you believe that your salvation lies in what you can do, not what God is offering you?

There is one more group in this allegory that bears a look. In all of the parables of the Kingdom as a banquet, there is no longer an exclusive list. We are in the time now when everyone is invited. That was the first dispute in the Church. To whom is the invitation sent? Is the invitation merely for a small group of people, or is the invitation for everybody? Matthew makes clear in this parable which side of the dispute he stands on. The banquet is for everyone. God's grace is given to anyone who will say "yes" to it.

That was the force behind the missionary movement. They wanted to get the word out. The missionaries were like the servants in this parable. They were to tell everybody. "God loves you, so come, come to the feast." They also preached, "You will be expected to bring a gift when you come, the gift of service." But for those who know the graciousness of the invitation, and the love of the one who sends it, that's no problem. It's done gladly, freely, and gratefully.

Can you imagine what it would mean to people who believe that my life is unworthy of such an invitation? Can you imagine what it would mean to people whose lives are burdened now with all kinds of problems, who think, "this is my fate in life?" To receive an invitation means that life is not about coping with problems all the way to the end. Life is about preparing for a banquet. That's the way you're supposed to live. Indeed, the banquet has already begun. So live that way. Live as if God's gracious invitation is to you, personally.

CHAPTER EIGHT

Who then is the faithful and wise slave, whom his master has put in charge of his household, to give the other slaves their allowance of food at the proper time? Blessed is that slave whom his master will find at work when he arrives. Truly I tell you, he will put that one in charge of all his possessions. Matthew 24:45-51

The Wicked Servant

*W*e most often vacation in the woods, away from so-called *civilization*. There is no television there, no newspapers. There's a radio, but you can't get anything on it except at night, and then you get everything in the world on it. There are a hundred stations trying to jam one little six-inch dial. It sounds like Babel.

There is a different rhythm to life up there, a rhythm set by nature, not the clock, and by human events, not business appointments: like a visit from a neighbor which becomes the highlight of the day, or a special meal with friends.

As a result of that I, for one, experience a kind of cultural shock when I come back onto "civilization." I guess you'd call it "re-entry stress," or maybe "the spiritual bends." The old ways set in again immediately, and I compulsively reach for a newspaper to find out what had been going on in the world while I was gone.

I am always shocked. The stories reveal the continuing corruption in high places, unspeakable crimes, and celebrity perversity. We get familiar, desensitized to such news because we are bombarded by the media on a daily basis. But when you step outside of this environment even for a short while, and reenter suddenly, you can see it vividly: How different we have become from the image we have of ourselves.

Instead of outrage, or at least embarrassment, at this corruption eating away at our common life, there is a prurient fascination with it. These stories are strung out day after day and explored in every detail.

After my last "reentry," the cover story in *Time* magazine is about the deterioration of the American character. The article focused on the phenomenon of special interest groups and nuisance litigation. How self-serving we have become, how narrow our vision of what America means.[1]

The story is illustrated by an interview that Peter Hart had with several teenagers. He asked, "What is it that makes America special?" There was silence for a long time, and then someone suggested, "Cable television." When they were asked, "How can we energize more young people to vote?" the answer was, "Pay them." Maybe we have to get away for awhile to see that we have changed. We are different than the image we have of ourselves.

Consider the biblical phrase: "When the Son of Man comes, will he find righteousness on earth?" That's from Luke, not the Gospel of Matthew, and it is paraphrased a little bit, but it is still appropriate. The Son of Man is the title given to the one who will come in judgment at the end of history. The phrase was probably used as a way of taking stock of where we are. To ask, "When the Son of Man comes, will he find righteousness on earth?" is to measure our life as it is against the way it is supposed to be. When the Son of Man comes, he will find immorality, injustice, corruption in high places, both in the private and public sectors, violence everywhere, violence to women, violence to children, crime in every level of society, and *greed*, which a former government official said is no longer considered a pejorative word in America.

When the Son of Man comes, what will happen? According

to the expectation, he will punish the evildoers, knock the tyrants from their thrones, cast the sinners into the outer darkness, and generally clean up the place. Our understanding of judgment has been shaped by prophecies of the Son of Man. The time of judgment will be a time of wrath against flagrant sinners.

The Parable of the Wicked Servant is a classic parable of judgment for it conforms to the expected pattern. But when I re-read it, it surprises me, and it may surprise you as well. It begins with a question. "Who then is the faithful and wise steward, whom his master has set over his household?" That's simple enough. This parable is about stewards, about stewardship. A steward is someone who has been given a responsibility, a mission to fulfill, a job to do. A steward is someone who works for someone else. "Blessed is that steward whom his master will find at work when he arrives."

The New Revised Standard Version translate *doulos* as "slave" rather than "steward." While literally accurate, *slave* creates a problem if we are sensitive to the way language is heard in various contexts.. In the first century slavery was a fact of life and therefore the word "slave" was not a problem to the reader. In our time, slavery is not only an anachronism, but the Christian faith is preached as a gospel of liberation. I fear many will not only misunderstand but will be offended by the word *slave*.

Since the function of the slave in the parable was to be a *steward,* I see the use of that word more helpful in getting to the heart of the story. Stewards are expected to do what they are commissioned to do. But that steward may say "Aha. My master is delayed," the old man isn't around any more, I can do what I want since there is nobody here to look over my shoulder to tell me what to do, or to reprimand me if I do something wrong." So he begins to mistreat other people and to live a life of profligacy and excess. When the master comes one day suddenly, he will "put him with the hypocrites, where there will be weeping and gnashing of teeth."

That's when I started to get uncomfortable, when I realized this parable is about trusted stewards, not gross sinners. The parable is addressed to the Church, not the world. The Church is those who have been given a mission to perform. We are the servants of the master, in the parable.

We're comfortable with that language. We use it all the time. It's the language of piety. We don't mind calling ourselves servants in relation to Jesus our Master. But I suspect that we gloss over what it means. According to this parable, when the master comes, he's not only going to judge those you read about in the newspaper, he's going to judge those who read the newspaper but do nothing about what they read there.

> *"He's going to judge those who read the newspaper but do nothing about what they read there."*

Their punishment is to join the hypocrites. Hypocrites are those who don't practice what they preach. Hypocrites are not those who try and fail. Persons who fail are Christians trying to live up to the highest standard that they know. They are human beings, so they're going to fail. They are like Paul, who suggested to the Philippians: I am not perfect. I haven't arrived, but I keep on trying. You're not a hypocrite if you keep trying.

Hypocrites don't try. They aren't even concerned about it. It doesn't occur to them that they should do anything about it. Hypocrites are those who want the blessings and the comfort of religion without the hard work and responsibilities. That's why *steward* is such an apt metaphor for the Christian. A steward is someone who is given a job to do and is expected to do it.

How many times Jesus talks about stewards! In fact, whenever he talks about what Christians are supposed to do, he uses the image of steward, or someone with a different title, like son, or servant, but who is asked to do something with the estate that the master has left with them.

The Parable of the Wicked Servant comes at the end of Matthew 24. The beginning of Matthew 25 is the Parable of the Bridesmaids, about those who have responsibility for keeping their lamps burning until the bridegroom returns. The faithful ones are those who take that responsibility seriously and make provision for a long wait. That's followed immediately by the famous Parable of the Talents, about stewards who have responsibility for taking care of the master's estate, or investing it. The faithful ones are those who do that responsibly, even at some risk. That's followed immediately by another parable, the Parable of the Last Judgment, known as the Sheep and the Goats, where those who take responsibility are the ones who do what Jesus told us to do. The unfaithful, the goats in the story, are the ones who say, we didn't know it was our job. We didn't know what to do. You didn't tell us what to do.

A Christian is the one who takes seriously what he or she is supposed to do in this world, and does it. A Christian is identified by his or her stewardship. Thus stewardship implies a certain degree of maturity. In these parables the master goes away and the steward is left on his or her own. You must now use your own judgment. You see what needs doing in this world and perform it according to your best understanding of Jesus' will.

Go back to the newspaper. Karl Barth, the great German theologian, who was one of the first to speak out against the rise of Hitler in the early 1930s in Germany, said, "Christians are those who hold the Bible in one hand and the newspaper in the other." I think he meant that the earth is the Lord's. This place belongs to God. The Church is called to be the steward of the world, both the natural and the social environment. The Bible is our job description, and the newspaper is the account of our stewardship. It lets us see how we are doing and what still needs to be done.

Our problem is acculturation. We get used to the world being the way it is; we think it's normal to be this way. Then soon we get implicated, have a stake in things staying the way they are, so we don't want them to change. Then two things happen, and you can generally divide Christians on this point. There are those, on the one hand, who put the Bible down because they say, it's foreign to my secular life, it's out of date, impractical in this kind of a world. And there are those who put the newspaper down because, they say, it disturbs my spiritual life, it's too worldly and I want to be spiritual.

But there is a third group: those who see themselves as stewards. They maintain the tension, as difficult as it may be. The Bible, they believe, is where we find our job description, what we are supposed to do, and the newspaper is the report of how we're doing.

God sends a prophet, whenever God wants the people to do something. Most recently Albert Shapiro, who, sounding like Amos the prophet from Tekoa, began an article by repeating what he had heard people say about America recently, how we are number one now that the Russian empire has fallen apart. There once were two superpowers, now obviously there is only one superpower. Now that we've won the Gulf war, suppressed a tyrant, and made it perfectly clear that we're not going to tolerate that kind of thing in this world. He agreed. It's obvious. We are now number one in the whole world.

> "*We are number one in the world . . .*"

We are number one in the world in the percentage of children living below the poverty line.

We are number one in the world in teen pregnancy.

We are number one in the world in murders of young males between the ages of 15 and 24.

We are number one in the world in murder by handguns of people of all ages.

We are number one in the world in the percentage of population in prisons.

We are number one in the world in the per capita consumption of energy.

We are number one in the world in polluting the earth.[2]

If the Church is steward over this place, both the physical and the social environment, and if one day we must give an account. I think I'd be uneasy.

So what do we do about it? Donald Messer, president of Iliff Theological Seminary, writes about the mission of the church in *A Conspiracy of Goodness*.[3] It is an appropriate title for that purpose because although the mission of the church hasn't changed, the world has changed, and therefore the strategy of the Church must change. In previous generations, even in America, where there is a separation of Church and State, the Church was at the center of things. It dictated the morality of the culture and served as its conscience. It exerted influence over all the institutions of society. The Church is no longer at the center, the Church is now on the periphery, which means if we are going to have an impact on life in our time, we must use a different strategy.

In the days when the Church was at the center of society, its role was to bless things, to give invocations before the world sat down to do its business. In the days when the Church is on the periphery, as it was in the first centuries, its role primarily is to convert the world, not to bless it, to change it, both its individuals and its institutions. And from the point of view of the world, that will appear as a "conspiracy."

The Church as a "conspiracy of goodness" is a model adopted by the European Church, and from which there have come a stream of anecdotes. Messer recalls that the revolution in Romania began when the nation rallied around a Hungarian pastor in that nation named Lazlo Tokes. He was an ethnic minority in that culture, a Hungarian, and the pastor of a Protestant church in a Catholic country. In almost every sense he was on the periphery.

One day the police came to remove him from his pulpit. The members of his church, along with the Roman Catholic priest and the Orthodox priest in that town, and some members of the Orthodox church as well, gathered to protest the police action.

One member of Tokes' church, a young man twenty-four years old, brought candles to hand out to the people. The candle had become the symbol of freedom in Eastern Europe. He lit his candle and began lighting the candles of other people there. That's when the police opened fire. They hit him, wounding him seriously. He was taken to the hospital where things worsened to the point where he had to have his leg amputated. Lazlo Tokes, his pastor, visited him there. The young man told him, "I lost a leg, but I am happy, because I am the one who lit the first light."

During the civil rights movement marchers would sing, "We Shall Overcome." They sang spirituals, they sang hymns of the Church, but they also sang: This little light of mine, I'm going to let it shine. This little light of mine, I'm going to let it shine. This little light of mine, I'm going to let it shine. Let it shine, let it shine, let it shine.

The song puzzled me, because it's a child's song. I sang it in Sunday School, and here were these adults, arms linked together, protesting injustice, risking their lives, singing a children's song. I learned it in Sunday School about the same time I was memorizing all those Bible verses, and I haven't sung it since.

Maybe that's what's wrong with the Church. Maybe we've forgotten what we learned in Sunday School. One of these days I think I'm going to write a book: *All You Ever Wanted to Know About Being a Christian You Learned in Sunday School,* including I have been given this news, this love, this commission, this job to do. I have been given this light, and I'm supposed to let it shine in the darkness of this world. "Blessed is that steward whom his master will find at work when he arrives."

CHAPTER NINE

The foolish said to the wise, "Give us some of your oil, for our lamps are going out." But the wise replied, "No! there will not be enough for you and for us; you had better go to the dealers and buy some for yourselves." And while they went to buy it, the bridegroom came, and those who were ready went with him into the wedding banquet; and the door was shut. Later the other bridesmaids came also, saying "Lord, lord, open to us." But he replied, "Truly I tell you, I do not know you." Keep awake therefore, for you know neither the day nor the hour. Matthew 25:1-13

The Wise and Foolish Bridesmaids

*T*he Parable of The Wise and Foolish Bridesmaids is about ten maidens with lamps who went out to meet the bridegroom. The bridegroom is delayed. Five of the maidens neglected to bring extra oil for their lamps; they are the foolish maidens. Five remembered; they are the wise maidens.

The bridegroom's delay is sufficiently long for all ten to fall asleep. At midnight there is a cry, "Here is the bridegroom!" All ten bridesmaids awake and rush to their lamps. During the long night all the lamps ran out of fuel, which is no problem for the wise maidens, those who have extra oil. It is a serious problem for the foolish maidens, who, in order to participate in the feast, must find fuel for their lamps. So at midnight they run to the stores, desperately trying to find a merchant who will open to sell them oil.

Meanwhile, the bridegroom arrived, and the parable ends with those who were prepared to go to the feast, and those who were not, left out. The tenth verse reads, "And the door was closed."

The next two verses, "Later the other bridesmaids came also, saying, Lord open to us. But he replied,' "Truly I tell you, I do not know you,'" are not considered by some critics to be part of the original parable. In fact, some say the parable itself lacks the literary characteristics to be an authentic Jesus parable.[1] (See Bernard Scott, *Hear Then The Parable,* 70-72). It is argued that such exclusiveness is inconsistent with Jesus' other parables in which those who arrive late are given a special invitation to come in. In the Parable of the Laborers in the Vineyard (Matthew 20:1-16) those who are hired at the last minute are paid the same wage as those who worked all day. Elsewhere Matthew offers the sayings about those who are last being first (Matthew 19:30, 20:16). The point of this Gospel is that God's grace transcends the distinctions we make between those who are worthy or unworthy, based either on merit or privilege.

Given the temptation of all human institutions to be exclusive, these critics suspect the eleventh and twelfth verses, which separate those who responded early on to Christian preaching from those who procrastinated until the *parousia,* represent the early Church, not Jesus.

If so, a word should be said about the scandal of exclusiveness in the Church. The most grievous instance is the "fencing" of the Lord's table.

First it is inconsistent with Jesus' radical message about the Kingdom in which those who arrive late are given a special invitation to come in. In the Parable of the Laborers in the Vineyard (Matthew 20;1-16), those who are hired at the last minute are paid the same wage as those who worked all day. Elsewhere Matthew offers the sayings about those who are last being first (Matthew 19:30, 20:16). In the message of the Kingdom, God's grace is inclusive and universal, therefore all are welcome into God's Kingdom, whether they come early or late.

The eleventh verse, "I do not know you. You cannot come in," might be the early Church speaking, not Jesus. It is the nature of human institutions, even the Church, to be exclusive, to take upon themselves the authority to decide who is worthy and who is not. While I suppose to some extent it is inevitable, and maybe even necessary, for institutions to make such distinctions in order to have definition and identity as institutions, we remind ourselves that it is not what Jesus taught about God's inclusive grace.

God's Kingdom is defined by the standard of God's grace, not our righteousness, and certainly not our judgment of other people's righteousness. So Jesus, to the utter horror of the leaders of the respectable institutions of his day, said all are welcome into the Kingdom. Prodigal sons are welcome. Latecomers are welcome. Foreigners are welcome. Street people, the homeless, sinners, publicans are welcome. Even religious people are welcome. We are all welcome.

Therefore nowhere does the Church give clearer evidence that it is a mere human institution than in its exclusiveness, and especially in its apparent lack of concern about its exclusiveness, and most especially at the Lord's table.

The Lord's Supper is the rehearsal for the feast of the bridegroom. It is the Kingdom feast, the heavenly banquet. Reserving the Kingdom for those who are like us is contrary to what Jesus taught. When the bridegroom says to the latecomers, "I don't know you; therefore you cannot come in," it sounds suspiciously like what a church would say to those whose beliefs or traditions differ from theirs. It's the Church "fencing the table." Jesus said, "Come unto me all you who labor and are heavy laden, and I will give you rest." "Go out to the highways and the byways and bring everybody in." "I have sheep who are not of this fold." Over and over again, Jesus preached inclusiveness, and over again the Christians practiced exclusiveness.

> "The Lord's Supper is the rehearsal for the feast of the bridegroom."

However, if one removes the troublesome verses eleven and twelve, one must still come to terms with verse ten: "The door was shut." It reminds us that the moral seriousness of Christian preaching should be emphasized as emphatically as Christian exclusion should be avoided. Our decisions have ultimate consequences. To say "no" to grace is not equivalent to declining to join an organization. It is electing not to enter the Kingdom.

For that reason alone, churches that have difficulty with the phrase, "The door was shut," while boasting of their inclusivity, should also make sure the invitation is heard by all. In the context of the parable, the eschatological dimension of the Gospel should lead to a disciplined life of preparedness.

Apart from these "critical issues," the parable speaks to a practical concern: "When will Jesus return in glory?"

The church had constructed a scenario in which Christ's first visit was like a preview of things to come, kind of a teaser. The next time he's going to bring the real thing, which will mean a decisive, radical recreation of the whole world, including all of nature. And next time it will be permanent, the Kingdom of God in all its glory, the real thing, as compared to this trial run, this dress rehearsal which concluded with his crucifixion and resurrection. Next time, the real thing. The question, therefore, is, when does it start? When will the Lord come?

Here's the answer. "Then the Kingdom of Heaven will be like this. Ten bridesmaids took their lamps and went to meet the bridegroom." Some were foolish to think that he was coming soon. Some were wise and were prepared for a long wait.

The bridegroom is delayed, so we are back to waiting on the Lord. To be Christian, this parable is saying, is to persistently wait on the Lord. There is a wonderful paradox here. He is not coming for a long time, so get ready. He probably won't return until long after we're gone, so be prepared for his coming any time.

That's the message, and it's crazy. If he's not coming for a long, long time, common sense would urge us to relax. Don't prepare. Give your attention to something else. Kick back, be comfortable. No! Get ready, be prepared, be alert. Have your lamps ready.

The parable concludes with the twelfth verse, "Watch. For you know neither the day or the hour." Watch. What's the purpose in watching? While they were waiting for Jesus to come at the end of history, he came now, while they were waiting. He didn't come in his final glory, he came as he came the first time, incognito. He came as he promised in the Gospel of John. "I will not leave you comfortless. I will come to you."

To say he comes to those who wait is to say he comes to those who expect him to come. It's as if he came not to end the vigil, but to join you in the vigil. To sit there with you as a friend comes to sit with you, make a pot of tea, just to be there, because a friend knows what it is like to wait; for the phone to ring with the news from the doctor; for the sorrow to ebb; for the pain to go away; for time to heal. Friends know it's a lonely vigil, so they come to be with you.

Simon Weil, a French Jew, was attracted to Jesus. Because of the war she was in exile, living in England while her fellow Jews were under persecution on the continent. She chose not to be baptized but to remain a Jew as a way of identifying not only with those of her own race who were suffering the Holocaust, but also to identify with Jesus, who was the outcast, the sufferer and the crucified.

She waited on the Lord in meditation, prayer and quiet. She wrote that while she was reading George Herbert's poem entitled "Love," it happened. Evidently she suffered migraine headaches, at which times she recited George Herbert's poem on love over and over again, clinging, she said, " . . . to all the tenderness it enshrines." She wrote, "I used to think I was merely reciting it as a beautiful poem, but without my knowing it the recitation had become, in fact, a prayer. It was during one of these recitations Christ himself came down and took possession of me."[2] "I will not leave you comfortless. I will come to you."

The Church said, be ready. Be prepared for a long, long vigil, but expect a visitation soon. Expect the Lord to come at the end, but be ready for his coming now.

They discovered another reason for waiting. Those who wait on God develop a quality of life that is recognizably distinct. I would like to say that it is distinctively Christian, but it is not. It is Christian, but it can also be seen in any religion that instructs people to wait on God. You can see it in Jewish spirituality, as represented in the words of Isaiah: "They who wait for the Lord shall renew their strength, they shall mount up with wings like eagles, they shall run and not be weary, they shall walk and not faith" (Isaiah 40:31). I've known such people. They have amazing strength. They are the people about whom you say, how do you do it? Where do you get the strength? They have the endurance of long-distance runners. I suspect in long-distance running endurance is only partly a matter of physical conditioning. It's also a matter of character, what we would call spiritual discipline. Character is when, wanting to quit, you endure the hardship and pain, accepting it as part of the race, hanging in there, keeping on going. Character describes both long-distance runners and those who wait on God. They can keep going and not get weary.

Most of us are willing to wait for something that we want. I'm willing to be patient if, in the end, I can be assured that I will get what I am waiting for: the job that I really covet, the spouse that I want, the end of this pain, or this loneliness, or this exile. I can wait for those things if I can be assured that the end of my waiting will mean I'll get what I want.

People who have waited a long time for what they want are often angry. They say, "I have waited long enough, longer than anyone has a right to expect me to wait, and it hasn't happened. Waiting has done no good."

> *"People who have waited a long time for what they want are often angry."*

Waiting on God is not like that. Waiting on God is not a scheme, a means of getting what you want, something you endure to earn a reward. Waiting on God is a way of life. It's not waiting for what I want; it's waiting to see what God will do. We don't know what God will do. We don't know how God will act, nor should we presume to tell God how to act. We wait, knowing neither the day nor the hour, confident that in God's own time God will act. That's waiting on God.

I came across evidence of it not too long ago in the writing of a theologian, of all places, and one with whom I don't always agree. In writing an article on how his mind has changed over the last decade, he concluded with this surprising confessional, revealing that he knows what it means to wait on God. This sentence gave it away. "We have all the time there is." Only a distance runner can say that. That's the statement of someone who has endurance. "We have all the time there is."

Then he added, "Whether I am in the middle of life's journey or at its end, it doesn't really matter. If I am in the middle I have arguments and projects in mind sufficient for a century. If the latter, the truth that has held the pieces together thus far convinces me all will be well."[3]

He concludes with these words of T. S. Eliot from his

poem *East Coker.* "For us there is only the trying. [We could say, for us there is only the waiting.] The rest is not our business."

More hopeful words were never spoken. "The rest is not our business." Unless they be these words: "Watch, for you know neither the day nor the hour."

CHAPTER TEN

> *For to all those who have, more will be given, and they will have an abundance; but from those who have nothing, even what they have will be taken away. Matthew 25:14-30*

The Talents

The English word *talent* can be traced back to the Bible, to the Parable of the Talents. In English a *talent* refers to a natural gift, like singing, or drawing, or dancing. But originally, and in the parable, a *talent* was a unit of money, a lot of money. A *talent* was a measurement of weight, equivalent to about sixty or seventy pounds, and used to measure silver.

So the master had left each servant a lot of silver, a precious legacy, a valuable estate. To one, five talents, over three hundred pounds of silver; to a second, two talents; and to a third, one talent, "each according to his ability," whatever that means.

The master is going on a long journey. The servants are no ordinary servants, they are money managers to whom the master has entrusted the future of his estate. They are professionals, so he doesn't need to tell them what to do. They know what to do. They have M.B.A.'s. Here is my estate, now make it prosper. Take good care of it. It is now up to the stewards, to these estate managers, those who have been given something precious and valuable, to decide on their own what to do with the talents.

The one with five talents traded them, earned five more talents, or a 100 percent increase in net worth. That's good. The second one, with two talents, did the same and realized a

100 percent increase. The third one, the one who had received only one talent, hid the money in the ground.

Matthew 25 consists of three parables. All three deal with accounting for your behavior after a long delay. The chapter begins with the Parable of the Bridesmaids, who are waiting for the delayed bridegroom. It concludes with the Parable of the Last Judgment, or "the sheep and the goats." The judgment, it says, will come "after a long delay." The Parable of the Talents is about a master who goes away and returns "after a long time."

Matthew is trying to make a point: Jesus' return to establish the Kingdom is delayed indefinitely, and it's probably going to be a long time before he returns. In between the times, between the time of his first coming and the time of his second coming, you are expected to be at work. When he returns he is going to ask only one question: What have you been doing with yourself? According to The Parable of the Talents, the question will take this form: What have you been doing with all that I gave you?

The third steward, the one who had one talent, hid that one talent, dug a hole in his yard, I suppose, and buried it under the rosebushes. We're surprised, maybe shocked at his behavior. It doesn't seem to us a responsible way to take care of such a large sum of money, seventy pounds of silver, especially somebody else's money. We have banks. You invest your money in banks for safekeeping. But then, considering what's happening to banks, maybe burying your money in the back yard is a better way of handling it. Under normal conditions, we would deposit our money in the bank. Therefore, we are surprised that a man entrusted with thousands of dollars would bury them under the rosebushes.

In Jesus' time, the opposite would have been expected. They were surprised not at the steward's behavior, but at the master's reaction. Burying treasure was a commonly accepted way of securing money in those days. Remember the parable Jesus told about the treasure hidden in the field?

That parable was effective because burying treasure was a common practice. Especially in times of crisis, or in times of war, people buried their money in fields, and since the world in those days had constant crises, many people left it in the ground. The steward was acting properly, and as expected.

All those hearing the parable in that culture would have praised the third steward and condemned the other two for dealing so recklessly with so great a sum of money. Five talents would have been worth tens of thousands of dollars, and it was somebody else's money. He put it all up on something. It had to be a high risk investment in order to get that kind of return. The hearers would have condemned that behavior as irresponsible, and would have praised the third servant's behavior as prudent.

It was common in what are called rabbinic tales, stories that the rabbis told, to refer to the Torah, the sacred Law, the five books of Moses, the precious heritage of Israel, as a treasure given to Israel to preserve. These parallels lead us to suggest that Jesus is referring to the Torah in this parable. In that case the question of the parable is, what do you do with it? What do you do with a religious heritage? Do you protect it or do you practice it?

Many in Jesus' time felt that faithful people protected their faith. For good reason. Over hundreds of years they had been under persecution. In the five hundred years since the end of the age of the great prophets, the mission of Israel had essentially been to survive, first in exile in Babylon, and then, through occupation after occupation of foreign armies, particularly the last two hundred years under the Greeks and the Romans. The Greeks were especially rapacious, even defiling the Temple, demeaning and desecrating the very heart of Jewish religion. It could be said that the Greek occupation threatened to exterminate the Jewish religion. Under those conditions it's no wonder, then, that the rabbis taught that to be religious, to be faithful, is to defend the faith, to bury it, as it were, hold onto it, hide it, protect it, so it will survive, and be passed on to the next generation.

Preserving, safeguarding, securing are the natural reactions of a religion (or an individual) that perceives it is under a threat. Perhaps Jesus is challenging that attitude about religion when the third servant is condemned, the one who buried the treasure, who did what a good Jew was expected to do. In a sense, Jesus was reviving the ancient prophetic tradition of Israel which flourished before these exiles and occupations began. The prophetic tradition was summarized in Micah's rhetorical question, "What does the Lord require of you but to do justice, love mercy, and walk humbly with your God" (Micah 6:8)? According to the prophets, you are expected to use your faith, walk with it, love with it, do it. Don't sit on it. Don't hide it.

> *"According to the prophets, you are expected to use your faith, walk with it, love with it, do it. Don't sit on it. Don't hide it."*

We remember that some scribes asked Jesus, "Are you one of the prophets?" He sounded like one. "Not those who say, 'Lord, Lord,' but those who do the will of my heavenly Father are my disciples." "By their fruits you shall know them," which is to say, you will know my disciples by what their lives produce.

Or, it's like a master on a long journey who is delayed. He entrusted his teachings to his disciples. Some lived by his teachings, applied them in their daily lives, invested them, as it were, in the world. Some merely talked about their faith, especially to those who believed the way they did. Sometimes they didn't even do that. They didn't do anything. They buried their faith, saying, "After all, religion is a private affair.

It's a personal matter. It's really something between you and God. Religion is to be there when you need it. So it's here, someplace, buried underneath all this stuff. Of course, I can't find it right now, but I know it's here someplace. At least I know where to look if I ever need it." That person doesn't fare very well in this parable. It's clear where Jesus comes out. Religion, he says, it not to sit on, or bury, or shelve, or can, or preserve, or even to pass to somebody else. Religion is to invest, use, spread, splurge, risk. So said a Texas "philosopher," Charles Jarvis. "Sitting in church doesn't make you a Christian any more than sitting in a chicken coop makes you a chicken."

> "Sitting in church doesn't make you a Christian any more than sitting in a chicken coop makes you a chicken."

That's what Jesus is saying in this parable. What I have given to you, this treasure, I have given to you to spend, use, invest in the world so that the world will be a better place.

Secondly, though Jesus identified the talents with the treasure of the Gospel, the Church immediately interpreted it in other ways, according to the situation where they found themselves. In a way particularly appropriate for our growing awareness of matters of ecology, they said the treasure is the bounty that we have received by God's grace from the Creation, and therefore all that we have is a gift to us from God.

The issue, especially in our time, has always been, Who owns this place? Who owns the earth? It makes all the difference in the world, you know, how you live in it. Who owns the earth? The Christian faith is absolutely clear about this, and the parables, especially this parable, and ones like it, are unequivocal: We don't own the earth. God owns it. What we have is on loan. Or better, it is under our stewardship until the master returns, at which time we will be asked one question: What did you do with what I gave to you?

The idea of stewardship, like the idea of talent, comes from the Bible, particularly from these parables. Stewardship governs our money, but more appropriately for what is going on in our world, it guides ecology.

It is part of our liturgical heritage to affirm that our life is dependent on God's gift, not our efforts.

> The earth is the Lord's and the fulness thereof.
>
> The heavens declare the glory of God,
> The earth shows forth God's handiwork.
>
> We give thee but thine own,
> Whate'er the gift may be:
> All that we have is thine alone,
> A trust, O Lord, from thee.[1]

Why is it so hard for us to apply these pious words to our daily life? Why it is so difficult for us to have a Christian ecology?

Lynn White, a scientist at UCLA, explained why Christians have been among the world's great polluters and exploiters of the earth. He wrote a famous essay in the 1960s when the ecological movement emerged, in which he blamed western civilization's exploitation of the earth on the biblical teaching of dominion. When human beings were created by God, they were told to have dominion over all the world. In his view that word *dominion* controls our attitude about nature, and leads us to look upon the rest of creation as something to dominate and do with as we please.

I don't deny how that has happened, but perhaps the Bible cannot be blamed for it. There is increasing, and convincing, evidence that other civilizations, even other religions, have allowed the rape of the earth. The problem is that we don't read the Bible. If we did, we would see that another message predominates: The earth belongs to God, not to us. We're not owners, not event when we have great holdings. We are stewards. The earth is not ours to exploit for our own needs. It is ours to manage as stewards for God, who will some day hold us accountable for this treasure, this beautiful green and blue jewel set delicately in space. Some day we will be asked, "What did you do with that treasure that I gave to you?"

> *"The Bible cannot be blamed for it. There is increasing, and convincing, evidence that other civilizations, even other religions, have allowed the rape of the earth."*

I came across a conversation between Knud Rasmussen and an Eskimo. Rasmussen, who died in 1933, for thirty years lived with and wrote about the Eskimos. He described the marginal nature of Eskimo life, how they are absolutely dependent on the reliability of nature; the short summer, the migration of animals, the thawing and re-freezing of the ice, the abundance of fish and seal. In order to survive in their hostile environment, all this must come in due season. But the Eskimo told Rasmussen, while they fear the cold and the other ravages of nature, most of all, "We fear the doings of the heedless ones among ourselves."

Fifty years ago this fear was heard as a curiosity coming from a primitive culture to an advanced civilization. Today it could apply to any culture in the world, including and especially ours which we call an advanced technological civilization. What we fear now are the doings of those who are heedless about these matters among ourselves, those who don't seem to care about the preservation of the gift that has been given to us, those who pollute the air and the water, those who ravage the earth and consume its resources needlessly.

In spite of efforts to convince ourselves that we are otherwise, we are just as dependent for our survival on the reliability of nature as the Eskimos. In fact, in our case we are more dependent on what could be called "the resilient mercy of nature," which takes all of the abuse that we inflict upon her, generation after generation, and, as e.e. cummings put it, "answers all of this abuse with spring"[2]—so far. We fear the cold, we fear the things we don't understand. But maybe more we fear the doings of the heedless among us.

The world is in danger, not because we have read in the Bible that we have dominion—a silly thought—but because we haven't taken seriously the biblical demand that the earth is the Lord's, and some day we will give an accounting for our stewardship.

Finally, the most common understanding of this parable is a reference to our personal lives. The dictionary defines a *talent* as a gift given to us to develop. That definition conforms precisely with the message of the parable. A talent is given to us to invest, to bring to fruition, to show some profit from.

It's probably also true that we bury our talents for the same reason that the steward in the parable buried his talent, out of fear. "I was afraid," he said, "so I went and hid your talent."

Around the church you will hear testimonies of those people who have heard the good news of the gospel and have changed their lives because of what they have heard. They decided that they were going to do now what they always felt they should do but didn't have the courage to do before, or were told that they were not worthy of doing. But Christian faith says to everyone, you are somebody. God has given you these wonderful gifts. It is up to you now to use them, invest them, bring them to fruition so that you can live the life that God intended for you in the Creation.

I hope you realize that not only is the gospel preached in church an important factor in that renewal of life, so are the personal words we say to one another. I have heard many people in telling their life story mention that it was the encouraging word of another, a parent often, who said, "You can become whoever you want to be. You should become whoever God intends you to be. You have the freedom to do that."

Most people never hear this liberating word. Communicated to most people from the time their first efforts are ridiculed, or just ignored, is that their talents are not worth very much, and they live their lives accordingly. Some of them live all of their lives as if they are not worth very much until, we hope, they come to church, and hear the liberating gospel of Jesus Christ, "You are a child of God. You are to be who God created you to be." In fact, the message is even stronger than that. The message of this parable is in the imperative mood. You must become who God created you to be, because some day you're going to be asked one question: "What did you do with all the potential that I gave you?"

In Praise of Imperfection: My Life and Work, is an autobiography written by a woman named Rita Levi Montacini, an Italian scientist. By looking back over her life as a scientist she is convinced that in research, neither intelligence nor efficiency are what really count. What counts is a tendency to underestimate difficulties, which causes one to tackle problems other, more reasonable persons say can't be solved.[3]

It's a wonderful lesson for stewards of Jesus' teachings. It is a lesson for stewards of the environment, who are told that there isn't anything we can do to stop the destruction of the planet. And it is for us as stewards of our own lives, when we are told that we are not going to achieve very much.

Invest anyway. Take what has been given to you and use it. See what happens. You will be surprised. What are you waiting for?

Notes

Chapter 1

1. Quoted in *The Tao Jones Averages* from Bennett W. Goodspeed (New York: Penguin Books, 1984), p. 85.
2. Robert Capon, *Bed and Board* (New York: Simon and Schuster, 1965), pp. 169-70.
3. Quoted in a review by David M. Lubin, *The Christian Science Monitor*.
4. "Conversation with Henri Nouwen," *Harvard Divinity Bulletin* (April-May, 1983), p. 9.

Chapter 2

1. Quoted in "The Triumph of Boris Pasternak" by Harrison Salisbury, *The Saturday Review*.
2. Quoted in Rushworth Kidder, "Say What You Mean!" *The Christian Science Monitor*, June 26, 1978.
3. Theodore Roethke, "Long Live the Weeds," *Collected Poems of Theodore Roethke* (New York: Doubleday & Company, Inc., 1966), p. 18.

Chapter 3

1. *The Los Angeles Times*, March 5, 1991.
2. Richard J. Mouw, "Humility, Hope, and the Divine Slowness," *The Christian Century*, April 11, 1990, p. 365.

Chapter 4

1. *The Complete Poems of Emily Dickinson*, Thomas H. Johnson, ed. (Boston: Little, Brown, and Co., 1960), Poem #1176, p. 522.

Chapter 6

1. David Mazel, "Old Friends and Small Family Wisdoms," *The Christian Science Monitor*, April 4, 1988, p. 27.
2. From an unpublished sermon by Bill Ritter, Farmington Hills, Michigan.

Chapter 7

1. "Seeing Too Much," an interview by Ken Adelman, *The Washingtonian*, July 1988.
2. Flannery O'Connor, *Wise Blood*, in *3 by Flannery O'Connor* (New York: New American Library, 1962), p. 64.

NOTES

Chapter 8

1. "A Nation of Finger Pointers," *Time*, August 12, 1991.
2. *Context*, 23:12, June 15, 1991, p. 5.
3. Donald Messer, *A Conspiracy of Goodness* (Nashville: Abingdon Press, 1992).
4. Ibid., p. 219.

Chapter 9

1. Bernard Brandon Scott, *Hear Then the Parable*, (Minneapolis: Augsburg-Fortress, 1989), pp. 70-72.
2. Lawrence S. Cunningham, *The Meaning of Saints* (San Francisco: Harper & Row, 1980), p. 67.
3. Richard Neuhaus, "Religion and Public Life: The Continuing Conversion," *The Christian Century*, July 11-18, 1990, p. 673.

Chapter 10

1. "We Give Thee But Thine Own," William W. How (1823-1897), in the *Book of Hymns* (Nashville: United Methodist Publishing House, 1964), p. 181.
2. e.e. cummings, *Collected Poems* (New York: Harcourt, Brace and Company, 1923), p. 21.
3. *Context*, 21:3, February 1, 1989, p. 1.